Lily Poetry Review

EDITOR-IN-CHIEF
Eileen Cleary

ASSOCIATE EDITOR
Christine Jones

CONTRIBUTING POETRY EDITOR
Lisa Sullivan

FLASH FICTION EDITORS
Mark Jednaszewski   Sarah Walker

VISPO EDITOR
Suzanne Mercury

ART EDITOR
Martha McCollough

MEDIA AND EVENTS
Rebecca Connors

READERS
Kay Bell, Julie Cyr, Konner Jebb, Elizabeth Mercurio, Chell Navarro, Tzynya Pinchback, Renuka Raghavan, Anastasia Vassos, Stacey Walker, Art Zilleruelo

COVER ART, ISSUE 6
Angel_35a by Ashley Parker Owens

© 2021. All rights reserved. This material may not be published, or reprinted without the express consent of the authors or artists attributed here.

drawings by Peter Urkowitz

CONTENTS

Natasha Pepperl	جون (Joon)	1
	Ceremony of a Relocation After a Fall	6
Natalka Bilotserkivets	Herbarium	7
	Lake	9
	Wine of the Lonely	10
Jennifer Franklin	Antigone Rememembers Her House in Massachusetts...	11
	Moemento Mori: Medieval Scribe	13
Dante Biss-Grayson	Untitled	14
Jim Willis	Local Mynas	16
Walter Lawn	Hawk	19
Miriam O'Neal	All Souls	20
Margarita Cruz	The Names We Used for God	21
Violeta Garcia-Mendoza	Leaf Shadow	22
Jenny Grassl	I Do Not Know How to Talk to My Fiancé	23
	How You Get Back Home	26
Amanda Hope	Wildlife, Sanctuary	28
	Aphasia	29
Richard Hoffman	Betrayal	30
	Fantastic Voyage	32
Ashley Parker Owens	Angel Series	34
Shelagh Powers Johnson	Jump	36
Lou Vargo	Leftovers	38
Jennifer F	Oranges	40
Barbara O' Byrne	Triangulation	43
Andy Smart	In Irons	45
Edward Kaitz	Spider Sun	48
Sam Cha	March 16, 2021	49

Sam Cha	The enemies address their makers and the sons of their fathers	50
	Oracles	51
Zedekiah Schild	Parachuting in a Lion Storm	65
M.J. Turner	Haddock	66
Adam Day	Expanse of Reality	67
Laura Reece Hogan	Heart as Siphonophore	68
Sharon Tracey	Driving up Haleakalā, House of the Sun	69
Jay Brecker	Albuquerque, NM: January 5, 2020	70
	Aleatory	72
Julia Lisella	I'm Receiving Now	73
Jennifer Barber	Foothills, Memorial	74
	Holbein's "Christ Lying in the Grave"	75
Sarah Deckro	Night Fountain	76
Jane Poirier Hart	A Day	77
	Fevered Is	78
Jonathan Aibel	Disappointments	79
Robert Wislon	Vitrectomy	80
JW Summerisle	bodkins	81
	unremarkably arboretum	82
	hordeum vulgare	83
Jason Montgomery	Imperial Rattler	84
Gloria Monaghan	Cormorant on the Strand	85
	Remnants of my Property	88
	A Place in the Sun	90
	Raintree County	92
David Dodd Lee	A Hateful Mob	93
Neil Silberblatt	Elegy for the Man of Steel	94
Jenna Le	My Happiest Times Have Been in Asian Restaurants	95

Libby Maxey	Okuribi	97
	Not Brought up for Waka	98
	A New Old Saying	99
Christie Page	Bug 2	100
Carla Drysdale	Before the Divorce	101
Frances Donovan	What a Mess I've Made	102
Eric Roy	All My Wins Are Going to Need Asterisks	103
Jennifer Martelli	Fascism	104
Willy Conley	Time Expired	106
	Dual Latches	107
Erwin Ponce	Binibini	108
Mid Walsh	On the Commuter Boat	109
Jennifer L. Freed	Surface	110
	As in a Window Glass	111
Anne Elezabeth Pluto	St. Francis Meets Mary Kay at the Prairie Pink Barbie Dream House	112
	Circle of Stars	112
	Sandy Texas Candy House	114
	We Started Out as Liars	115
Meggie Royer	Noah Leaves the Ark	116
K.T. Landon	This Is Not the End of the World	117
Stephen Nelson	Pages from *Asemic Tantra*	118
Heather Nelson	Review: *Petition* by Joyce Peseroff	123
Andy Smart	Review: Stephen Kuusisto's *Old Horse, What Is to be Done?*	126
Lisa J. Sullivan	Review: *The Dandelion Speaks of Survival* by Quintin Collins	129
Lisa Allen	Review: *Hue & Cry* by Diane K. Martin	132
J.D. Scrimgeour	Review: *All Morning the Crows* by Meg Kearney	136
Eric E. Hyett	Review: *Unholy Heart* by Grace Bauer	139

Jennifer Martelli	Review: *Loosen* by Kyle Potvin	142
Kali Lightfoot	Review: *The Taste of the Earth* by Hedy Habra	146
M. P. Carver	Review: *Pelted by Flowers* by Kali Lightfoot	149
Neil Leadbeater	Review: *Ash* by Gloria Mindock	151
Carol Hobbs	Review: *The Animal at Your Side* by Megan Alpert	154
Kirsten Miles	Body as Blade, a review of *Divine Divine Divine* by Daniel Summerhill	156
Gloria Monaghan	Review: *Manimal Woe* by Fanny Howe	159
Eileen Cleary	Review: *The Land of Mild Light* by Rafael Cadenas	164

Contributors Notes   166

NATASHA PEPPERL

جون (Joon)

I. جون (joon)

My grandmother offers *joon* as a great unfolding,

as her backyard buzzes with dozens of deep-rooted

rosebushes pressing dry June with a knowing of garden

hose or the *ghormeh sabzi* she laces with pinto beans

and Persian limes and simmers nearly sweet, served

with *tadig* she makes sweat gold

olive oil and saffron, a bowl of raw green

onions to peel back each layer of my soul.

How to say: my blood will always carry

your fingerprints?

II. جان (jâne)

My sister and I take turns rocking

a red-headed doll while murmuring baby

jâne. One suburban friend — they are all

white and cool as our bedroom walls— asks

why we've named the doll Johnny when, clearly

it's a girl?

The doll's name is Carol, but we have

no languageable answer. Doesn't everyone coo

jâne to their babies? How else will they know

they're loved?

III. جونم (joonam)

Saying *joonam* requires a lip

pucker, like having my uncle

as an uncle requires a recurring nightmare

in preschool and kindergarten: I sit

on a standard 90s patio chair, all white

hard plastic, pinning eyes shut as a man

unfurls fingers up-down-across my tiny body,

It tickles, but if I laugh —

he'll kill me.

IV. جان (jân)

Sometimes my mother is silky as turkish

delights or the rising and falling *miges* and *ehs* she uses

on the phone with her mother and sister *jân*

or my pantless bottom spread

across her legs to meet the sting of kitchen utensils, how she uses a knife

edge to slide sliced onions into a pot for a thick stew.

I never remember the Farsi word

for mother, but I always remember *baleh,*

               baleh,

                  baleh.

V. جانم (jânam)

I'll keep *jânam* for myself, the moment my soul rose

to become her own mothering, worn

of the way my mother sucks back

nourishing, the moment my body filled

gathering waters for a new

joon, the moment before I knew of this swelling —

stiffening at my mother's greedy

touch, my skin — a river

already receding.

Note: There are no English language equivalents of the Farsi terms of endearment joon *and* jân *or their derivatives. When used among family members — especially when an older family member is addressing a child — these words insinuate a willingness to die for the other person as well as an acknowledgment that the other person is a part of themselves. Loosely translated, these words mean soul/my soul or life/my life or dear/my dear.*

NATASHA PEPPERL

Ceremony of a Relocation in Fall

After Donika Kelly

The sun reaches through the bare
window and fingers the cardboard
boxes and wakes us early.

The boy sleeping downstairs
stacked and carried all the boxes
inside with my husband.

Now the boy is lying
in the dirt of a field we see the tattered
edge of on our front porch.

Now the boy is an unopened
box lying in a hospital bed
with a swelling head.

Now the boy has been opened
— a harvest. Someone lies

with his lung, another with his heart,
somebody with his right eye

as the sun reaches through
the bare.

NATALKA BILOTSERKIVETS

Herbarium

There's nothing better than the scent
of a child's hair—only a dried violet
smells like that, only the petals
of a bluebell on its delicate stalk neck,
two lightly joined leaves
like shoulders.

The best is almost imperceptible
because it's shy: a smell, childhood
or even, death—
though its rest is so sweet,
so exacting.

Yesterday he was reading and drawing,
today he played a little basketball,
the clarinet. Hundreds of ordinary matters
have bored him a little. Most often
he thinks about barefoot wanderings.
The wind drills a whistle tunnel
in the cosmic blue.

Will God take grain on his journey
to harvest some rice or wheat?
Will he stow together in his pocket
a small beast and an innocent bird
to restore the breed on new
unseen land of this earth
and, like a trophy on a table,
offer a human being as a reward?

But more often his hand,
like a boy's or, perhaps, an old man's,
pauses on a thick folio
in a leather cover where life
has neither weight nor feeling,
nor even sense. Where the thin paper
exposes other paper,
dried cereals, leaves, and flowers,
beauty as memory, as secret doors,
a game in smells and lost thoughts.

translated by Ali Kinsella and Dzvinia Orlowsky

NATALKA BILOTSERKIVETS

Lake

Ferns embody the lake's shore.
No—there's only a white face. Grow,
you, semicircular, round—swift,
suppressed cry of loneliness.

You—in the dark fern—a glass lens from sky!
I see you lying face down in the grass.
Earth around you smells
like a hive; the lake of shores

in the living soul…How freely
new blood rocks in veins,
wind of wave, wave in the wind—
evenly, evenly, evenly, and again.

translated by Ali Kinsella and Dzvinia Orlowsky

NATALKA BILOTSERKIVETS

Wine of the Lonely

for Antanas A. Jonynas, Lituanian poet (b. 1953)

Recalling this place and time, they
stood together in one line. Neither
a horse's nor dog's shadow nor loneliness
could cast a boundary
between them.

They breathed each other's breath,
but knew nothing of one another—
unable to find the distance
to know.

Ripe dandelion fluff,
and the juice of its stem
flowed inside their veins.
A carved old nettle leaf
lay on their hearts.

An intoxicated butterfly
flew the length
of their locked bodies
from end to end—
but couldn't break
free to the meadow green.

translated by Ali Kinsella and Dzvinia Orlowsky

JENNIFER FRANKLIN

Antigone Remembers Her House
in Massachusetts at the End of the Last Century

Even without moonlight, I still see

the two brown horses standing

by the fence across the road.

In late summer, grass grows tall

around the posts. For weeks,

I did not leave except to unlatch

the mailbox and walk with the black

and white dog back to the empty

yellow house. Those rooms watched

ghosts fly from the bodies of the living.

Those fields opened to take bulbs

from my hands. Pine trees admonished

the creek as a turkey vulture emerged

and frightened the dog on the deck.

In the spring, flowers clustered

in small patches. Tulips top-heavy

with shame, tipped in the wind.

One owl watched from the broken elm.

 The moon remembers the waif I was

and watched my wrist pull the red

damask curtains closed for the night.

JENNIFER FRANKLIN

Memento Mori: Medieval Scribe

She toiled in silence on manuscripts. Maybe
in a scriptorium with a view of green,
a splash of white for sheep or cloud,
depending on the season. She presided
over her paints whose colors, to her,
were more like words. When archeologists
find lapis lazuli between her teeth
they prove women, too, illuminated manuscripts.

Imagine her kneeling at a wooden table—
in candlelight, at dawn, drawing the tip of the fine
brush through her lips to make it finer still. Listen
to her sigh, as her open mouth cradles ultramarine
that will hide in the cracks of her teeth for centuries,
blue as a pharaoh's death mask. Deep as angels' robes.

DANTE BISS-GRAYSON

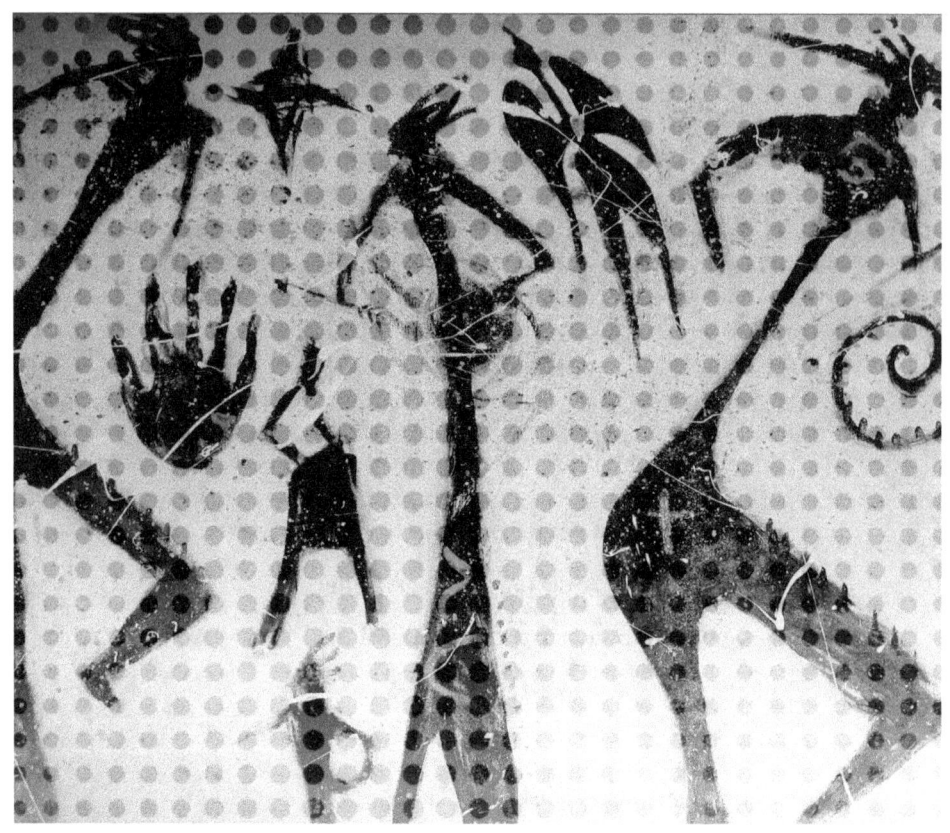

Untitled

JIM WILLIS

Local Mynas

I

The Kona sunset exhausted the mynas.
They saw thirty-seven discrete reds,
twenty degrees of sulfurous yellow,
and several flashes of polarized rose

which triggered a debate about color and light
as they gathered chattering in the banyan tree.
Eventually beaks nestled into feathers
as sleep came mercifully to the colony.

Then it was all right to dream,
if that is what mynas really do,
for surely someone kept the watch,
though all the birds were night blind.

II

The moon rose like a candled egg
alarming one myna in the roost
unnecessarily it seems
for there was no feral cat.

The cats see well at night but believe
the flock becomes one big bird
with two enormous yellow beaks
and eyes that look front and back.

Mynas have a yellow triangle of skin
above each eye shaped like a beak.
A feral cat knows not to try
to surprise a bird so circumspect.

III

I have seen the birds in daylight,
right-sized again on public lawns,
Janus-faced, one beak on a bug,
the other engaged with all of heaven.

Brought here like the Portuguese
to work the sugarcane fields,
they ate a plague of armyworms,
who also came from somewhere else.

When the birds left the sugarcane fields,
they set out like the Portuguese
to live freely among the natives
and walk about as *kama`āina*.

The two-faced birds were like two birds--
the one fighting all day over territory,
the other gathering to chat at sunset
in the Indian tree of enlightenment.

WALTER LAWN
Hawk

First the thump and shriek,

Then – memory catching up –

The plunging streak, swift

As a thrown stone, then

The great bird, ponderous,

Beating its way upward,

Squirrel in its talons.

Then our son, in surgery.

Then your prayers

Rising in empty air.

MIRIAM O'NEAL

all souls

my sister and her wife arrive

and I ask them to help me accomplish

something for the living

            but they keep laughing and looking elsewhere—

at the oriole nest that swings in a crook of the yellowwood

            and the brittle birch leaves on the patio that have refused

to begin to rot in the drench of All Soul's rain

I am invisible   I see it now   I am the portal

they've passed through   to be here

they used to come through my door on Christmas Eve

laden with crockpots of chowder and sausage

           raucous with love

 in the morning I tell the dog

about their visit and he wags his tail

which makes sense

           they loved him too

MARGARITA CRUZ

The Names We Used for God

Margarita like Daisy
like the perennial,
like I will always return.
Nana's harsh tongue, a bottle opener,
and all of the names we didn't use
when we called for god instead
manzanilla y menta y la yerbero on the corner.
Sometimes Nana and never Jesus because he moved
across la frontera and never looked back
like my uncles and sisters and eventually me.
When my uncle died, it meant
his body would never return home
where it would never be buried.
That night blue and red turned the sky purple
by force against a grey backdrop
On my father's birthday
on father's day
on the day my tío became tierra,
the dirt and dust
that never returns.

VIOLETA GARCIA-MENDOZA	Leaf Shadow

JENNY GRASSL

I Do Not Know How to Talk to My Fiancé

                                        years' hands of sand to fortress

                              now clock the rough

                                            my island slipping   to his sea

                                                      did he know his mother

                                would throw his full urn at the tide

    and our twenties

              two cakes   groom's dark rum and fruit

                     bride's sea-foam-icing white   ordered   I tasted sudden smoke

of baseball leather and his skin

                         cardiac arrest's landfill wedding

                 invitations

        as to his rest   I had no say   no ballpark   stood in the door of wife

he is the only one I ever knew

        who did not like the ocean

             the hair on his neck would wake

                   as from somnambulance

sea married

I partook of pleasing

numbers in a shell   mapping chambers

losing the bell

of the surface buoy

to a benthic howl

          his particulate ash

          now parts per oblivion

                                      his body rides
                                      every wave   drops

                                      to the abyssal plain

                                        stars brittling

    where arteries narrow   where my joints join

    harder   he disperses farther

No grave clay of his pitcher's mound   and I don't know

        the scores this year

what bright cap might uncover him

my then-love,

> *terra firma our first date   you know the zoo   some pelts survive the animals   they do not long to cinder   hung in a keeper's den   mouthing last moments   e v e n closed lips casket stain root-split silk of yours I could give voice to   a keeper e a r t h the burn is just over   and over   do you hear   each always squall   gull mewl and long   staircase of my whelk-buried cry*

JENNY GRASSL

How You Get Back Home

seek preternature of the woods

        the light short   like cake

    long on butter   and going fast

              moss soft in its crypt of rock   crevassed

                      to get there   a rocking horse

                            and an offer of wooden apples

        follow the crack   widening

ride into perforated shade spangling

        acquire crow gleam before dark

            land on your porch crescendo rising

     breaching walls and open doors

                the repeat   of a man's Wagner heart

        drags cricket song

  your winged Valkyries' ride

    song of women not trifling

        choosing the dead for a heaven

    you know you could but he owns the sound

watch through rusted screens

            because you always wandered off

                you must carry a tender ruin

AMANDA HOPE

Wildlife, Sanctuary

The animals that you've taken

Out of your poems huddle around me.

The things they mean live in them like parasites.

They cannot return to the wilderness, all imprinted

With your troubles and obsessions as they are.

They flick their ears, still listening

For your urgent way of making sense of things,

Expecting your clutch of knuckles in their fur.

How they sprang unbidden from your mind

In your desperations. How you sent them away

When they got too big for you to comfortably

Keep, like the leopard cub you hid until too late.

AMANDA HOPE

Aphasia

mirrors of that bright

kaleidoscope, language

smashed

leaving you   colors

but no pattern

that workaday

badger   its jaws

falling open to reveal

an egg

yet unbroken

to maybe hatch

and call out

some chirp or whistle

which I will

(I promise)

whistle back

RICHARD HOFFMAN

Betrayal

> *One's-self I sing, a simple separate person*
> — Whitman

Earth's tragicomic bricolage,

    I am imagined

of necessity and desire — oh,

and fear; mustn't forget fear.

So I see angels

jutting from corbels and cornices,

their appearance

        suggested by air conditioners

        high above the avenue

    as the planet

reaches combustion temperature

and a bit of friction here or there

        burns down a city:

people reading, playing, cooking, sleeping,

sharing their innocent puzzlement,

  telling one another their neighborly lies

        while shrieking mirror

     neurons split the atoms

belonging to me, belonging to you.

Corruption runs in the gutters

    and celebrates itself,

laughing, and only mildly ashamed.

Now everyone can see the future

    as if possessed

of powers they never had before,

        though most refuse.

My country, 'tis

    a giant clock

above a loud arena of applauding victims,

    and children without the choice

        not to believe.

RICHARD HOFFMAN

Fantastic Voyage

1.

Like one of the characters from that old matinee, I am inside the heart

but somehow it is my own heart and I am inside a humming room, waiting

before a round door I know to be a valve that will admit a flood of the past,

a forceful torrent of what is depleted, the valve like a spaceship's airlock,

and before I open it I must unlock the corresponding valve in the far wall,

which I understand is the future, and stand back, or history will drown me.

2.

There are these griefs, you see, starved, desiccated as the tiny corpses

of insects left in abandoned webs that quiver with my movements,

here in this creaky attic or cellar, someplace I don't visit often

enough to recognize the things I have piled there haphazardly.

Anything of worth I ever found here I found looking for something

else among the things I chose to store away for some other, easier life.

3.

 Inside me are places where conclusions and confessions are conjecture

because the dead have left behind them a film of sticky shame

and a granulated record of deeds and misdeeds like the residue of sleep

around the eyes each morning. *Merrily, merrily, merrily, merrily* I pull

the cord to try to start the engine but my little boat drifts downstream

toward the falls highlighted on the map. Maybe it won't be so bad.

ASHLEY PARKER OWENS **Angel 131a**

SHELAGH POWERS JOHNSON

Jump

The story begins like a closed fist, tight and finite. The facts are simple, unchanging. It happened how it happened; no need to wonder. But over time, the fingers begin to uncurl, stretching and searching, as if maybe there is more to know—as if maybe the past is a malleable thing. And then the hand opens, flattens, the palm like an offering: I have a story for you.

No one noticed when he slipped away from the party and up to the hosts' bedroom. He took his shoes off, tucked them in a corner; he left a half-drunk beer on the bedside table as if he might come back for it later. It's hard to say what compelled him to do what he did next: maybe he didn't know the pool had been drained for the winter and the jump was nothing more than a misguided party trick, something to liven things up; maybe from the second story window the tarp thrown over the hollow ground had looked soft and inviting, a cushion to break his fall, to scoop him into its folds and toss him up and away; maybe the darkness below had been a welcome mouth, the beast he'd been seeking to swallow him whole.

A picture of his wife had surfaced on the internet a month before, an artsy shot with the blurred hint of nakedness, the camera focused in on her face so you could see the lines that had begun whittling their way around her eyes and mouth. It had seemed like an odd injustice, this mildly erotic picture being so unflattering—maybe he'd felt a sliver of sadness for her tucked somewhere beneath his own anger and hurt. It hadn't been their bed she was on; it hadn't been him behind the camera. Still, maybe he wished she'd looked beautiful. Maybe then the world would have been kinder to them. Maybe then the sidelong glances would have been edged with jealousy rather than pity, rather than with disdain. If she'd been young, her hair a silky gold that didn't glint with silver, her body an invitation rather than an apology—maybe then everything would have been different.

After the jump, there were weeks of quiet. The rumors slowed; the picture stopped flashing across cell phone screens; there were no more snarky captions. Instead people brought her tuna casseroles and frozen lasagnas, a gift certificate for a maid service, for a massage, for a year of free oil changes. She was cradled in the soft palm of sympathy while whispers about what she had done, about why he had jumped, were stifled within a balled fist, closed but ready to punch. She couldn't be both a widow and a whore, so for a little while she was armored by her grief.

But tragedies turn stale in the open air—they need dark corners and the wet must of secrets, edges that morph in the shadows. People need to have a story to tell, a handful of truth to work between their fingers until the facts bend into new angles. They need to burrow deep into the comfort of other people's mistakes, curl themselves around the dimpled flesh of these imperfections, imagine the jump again and again to remind themselves that they are still whole.

LOU VARGO

Leftovers

     Nylons, makeup, hair, lipstick. That's been her routine for over twenty-five years if she so much as steps foot outside the house. She did it during the war when she worked at the plant and all the men were overseas. She's done it all the years since, while Louie and their seven older kids wore away every other part of herself that she loved. Today is no exception. When she's ready, she puts her little Louis in the stroller, her purse in the diaper bag and walks to the bus stop. It's summertime and she feels her sweat catch the soot that Zug Island's steel mill belches a few blocks away. The diaper bag hangs heavy off her shoulder. The stroller presses hard against her palms. She pushes.

     When the bus arrives she drops the coins into the tall rectangle and little Louis hands the driver a nickel for the transfer downtown. The stroller smacks with an awkward *ping* or *thud* into seats and kneecaps on the way to an empty seat in the back. They get out at Hudson's Department Store and she pushes the stroller across the wide sidewalk to the entrance. The tall glass doors whoosh open with a sound that startles the boy. He looks up at the vast space, mouth open and eyes wide.

     Once inside it's as if a puff of cool air lifts her off the marble floor while "Claire de Lune" plays inside her head. Looking up, the soft light from the high ceiling reminds her of a picture she saw once of a yellow field of tickseed in morning sunlight, muted and unfocused. She realizes that it was on her doctor's office wall, over his shoulder and just past his words. She was looking at it when she heard "toxemia," when she realized that she and her little Louis inside had to check into the hospital, and "Yes – immediately."

     The music in her head stops. It's replaced by the foreign sounds of gentrified shoppers. She's back on her feet, pushing now. The cool air isolates the sweat in her armpits and under the thick wires of her bra. The press of her palms against the stroller returns. Sales people turn away and the shame of not belonging grows inside her chest like a tumor. She heads to the escalator and down to where she came to shop.

     Hudson's basement is humid and ancient. She feels better here. The shame is less panicked and more familiar. It's the shame of knowing she belongs. The harsh light flatters nothing, turning everything it touches to a soft splotchy mass that looks like unbaked bread. The windowless walls are nicotine yellow and the tile floors are scuffed.

The clothes down here are a sea of wrinkled orphans struggling to find their place among resealed boxes of random shit all piled on peeling Formica tables. Among the piles she finds four blouses and a blue pantsuit. She holds each piece up to her neck in a mirror near the bathrooms. She gently shushes Louis and smiles small when she gets to the pantsuit. The color is good and the cut will help hide her weight. She double checks the price and drapes the pantsuit over the stroller. She pays at the register, snapping each bill between her thumb and middle finger, making sure she doesn't hand over two precious bills for one.

Back outside the heat is punishing. She pushes the stroller to Lafayette's Coney Island five minutes away. She and Louie used to come here when they were dating. Now it's her excuse to keep from having to go home to him. She scrapes some fries onto Louis' tray. The crunch of raw onions on the Coney dog is familiar and feels good between her dentures.

****

Later with her makeup, nylons and lipstick still on, she'll rewarm the pot roast and open a can of pork and beans for Louie and the kids. She'll stare at the cube of fat floating inside the can's brown liquid and when she dumps it into the pan it'll remind her of her baby's shit as it spreads across the bottom.

She'll stand over the stove and see herself as she was before; when she would swallow the days whole like a pill and its energy would radiate from her strong body out to the bigger world she could still only imagine. The moment will end when little Louis screams and runs to hug her leg. She'll turn off the burner and put the leftovers on the table.

JENNIFER F

Oranges

Rick bought the oranges for one dollar a pound. He bought fifty pounds.

"That's too many," Pam said. "Two people can't eat all those oranges."

"It's a good deal," Rick said.

Pam ate them, alone, when the house was dark. For a week, she ate oranges every night until her stomach was taut with pith and seed. Their scent hung in the house like a miasma.

The following week she brought an orange to her neighbor Bill. To bring two would be too obviously profligate. "Thank you for the orange," Bill said, and invited her in for a drink. After gin rickeys he peeled the orange in one long, curling strip, then stacked the peel on the coffee table so it took the shape of an orange again. To Pam it seemed to snap into place, perfect and whole.

Pam began bringing oranges to her meetings with Bill. Sometimes he would put small trinkets inside the empty peel, a chocolate truffle or a note that said "Hello," before handing it back to her. Sometimes she would rub the peel, zest side up, on his body before they began lovemaking in earnest. This was easily construed as sensual but was intended to cover up his musty smell.

"Where do these oranges come from?" Bill asked at last.

"I have a tree," she answered, too quickly to stop herself. There was no real reason to hide who bought the oranges — Bill knew about Rick, and vice versa. Whenever she was in bed with someone, however, she had the notion that it was a matter of etiquette to adopt the pretense that they were the only living beings in the world.

So she told Bill she had a tree that grew outside her window, close enough that she could pick oranges in bed. She described honey-scented flowers that bloomed even when the tree was in fruit. The next time Pam came over Bill asked her to tell him about the tree again, timidly, like someone admitting a harmless but mildly unsavory fetish.

She embellished the image, adding thick leaves that cast shadows like old lace, an aroma like the hair of a nubile girl, a community of songbirds whose music resembled Brahms if you listened in the right state of mind. With every visit he asked for more. Soon she was shouting details about the tree's beauty and fecundity in the midst of their lovemaking, while he thrashed beneath her.

She relished in it more than she expected to.

It became harder to walk across the street to her own house, with its air full of oranges. It nauseated Pam, and Rick's touch made it worse. He did his best to help: he bought various aids online and presented them like men present jewels in old films. They each tried on masks: big-eyed girls from erotic cartoons, latex presidents, grinning animals. The oranges penetrated all of them.

It was after Millard Fillmore and Buchanan that Rick became especially frustrated. He tossed his mask into the corner, where it collided with an orange. "Fucking Whigs," he said.

"It's alright," Pam said, patting him.

Rick leaned into her, then lifted his head. He had an idea: a threesome. Did she know anyone who would be interested?

"I might," Pam said. "He lives nearby."

Bill agreed, and Pam and Rick set about gathering what they needed: dinner (roast chicken and seasonal vegetables), wine, some mild hallucinogens. They cleaned the house thoroughly, though they gave up on getting rid of the orange smell.

Pam visited Bill the night before to make sure he had no aversion to the menu. He was jittery with excitement. "Are you looking forward to seeing Rick?" Pam teased.

"No, the orange tree," Bill said. He ran through Pam's inventions: the songbirds, the nubile scent, the heavy fruits. She did not remember telling him these details. Her palms sweat so much she left before touching him.

It was dark by the time Pam got back to the house. In the yard she scratched out a hollow and poured in the remaining oranges. One day was not much to grow a tree, but the more seeds she planted the more likely one would sprout. All she wanted was a shoot she could show her neighbor — an exaggeration was better than a lie.

The dinner was a success, though the chicken was slightly pink. After dessert they steeped the tea in a stoneware pot Bill had brought. It was a pleasant blend; along with the psilocybes were dried ginger and rooibos. The wine had an immediate effect, however. Soon they were fumbling into bed.

"Would you like to try on a mask?" Rick asked Bill, holding out a Coolidge.

"No, thank you," said Bill. There was no need.

"I think the tea isn't as mild as the guy told me," said Rick.

"Oh man," said Bill, from the back of his throat. "Look at that."

Pam saw an orange tree, enormous enough to demand the full range of perception, its branches bent almost to breaking with flowers and fruit. Relief cascaded through her body, more powerful than any orgasm: the seeds had sprouted.

"That's something," said Rick.

For the moment, they were satisfied.

BARBARA O'BYRNE

Triangulation

At thirteen, us girls pony; men bounce on the moon. Our suburban world is symmetrical lawns, split levels, and Dairy Queen. Vietnam is something on TV, an American thing. Facts are true. Anyone can look them up. The talk is all football at our Catholic high school. Our team, the Saints, (what else?) assumes mythic proportions. Pep rallies, special assemblies, busses to transport us to and from games. We bathe in the glow of district and city trophies in the school foyer. Elisa, senior cheerleader of the football team, is pissed. Her squad can't go to the team victory party. "Boys only," the principal informs her. In the corridors between classes, in the cafeteria at lunchtime, in the foyer at the end of the day, she airs her suspicions, "He's a perv. That's why he doesn't want girls there." Her meaning? It's another Vietnam. But I laugh along with the other girls, mimic her, mock her. She's just mad she can't go to the party. Rumors circulate about her. The next year, Elisa's gone. Who knows where? Who cares?

****

I am eighteen and fluent in Freud and Marx. No one dances; everyone is stoned. We are passionate about classless societies, the dispossessed. We get it. We question everything. On Thursdays after class, we gather in the office of a young part-time instructor. Leon tells us about the suburban high school students he taught for a few years. "Vacuous," he says, "they have no consciousness to raise." James says he's heard that LSD in the suburban schools is an epidemic, fed from the pockets of affluent parents, a sign of the nihilism bred by corporate capitalist culture. I am about to say that I attended that school and to agree with James when Leon's face contorts in anger. "At St. Joe's, the drugs are not the worst of it. You've heard about that famous football team. The Saints? Shiny trophies and regular write-ups in the city papers. But have you heard about those players-only parties? No trophies are worth what is done to those boys. Heinous acts!" I am mute. I have discovered this other Vietnam. I know what Leon is implying. But did he really say it? Anyway, I have a term paper due tomorrow and I am busy inventing myself.

****

I am twenty-three and the women's movement is in full swing. Fridays are social nights at the Women's Center where I volunteer. Women of all ages swirl around Good Will couches and coffee tables, nibbling from vats of free popcorn and $.50 cans of beer and $.10 cans of soda. Disco music blares. A newcomer is excitedly talking to one of the regulars, pausing only for long swigs on a Molson. She is a solid woman, maybe thirty-five, with chin-chopped-brown hair, flecked with silver. Her full moon of a face is dominated by hard gray eyes. She reminds me of a medieval woodcutter. A pudgy, short-haired dog curls at her feet, tucking its head over her crossed ankles. My friend, Jennifer, offers some information. "That's Dani. Don't let her corner you. I heard her story twice at the Take Back the Night Conference, once when she was sober and once when she was drunk. She's a teacher who got fired two years ago. Pretty clear why when you see the way she's knocking them back." I nod, and move on to other friends.

Later that evening, I sink into one of the sofas that reek of cigarettes, grime and beer. Dani plops into the empty spot beside me. "Have you met Max?" she says hoisting the small black dog in her arms. "He's a rescue." It's clear she wants to talk. She's a few beers along and launches into her story. She tells me she had been a teacher at St. Joe's in the suburbs but now is looking for a job in the city. I don't tell her I went to that school. I am looking for an escape route. Dani unpacks the tale of how her teaching career was sabotaged by the principal. "He had it in for me," she begins, "constantly spreading rumors that I was an alcoholic, unfit for the classroom." Dani's tone shifts between a detached, disjointed rambling, her eyes looking outward to an invisible audience, to an in-your-face rant, her steel gray eyes widening, glowering. Dani attracts a group. She raises the volume, "Those players were being messed with. Everyone knew. Nobody said anything. Nobody wanted to hear about it." She reaches down for the small dog who is whimpering on the floor and cradles him in her arms. I make an early exit from the center.

****

I sit in my dark 2/12 apartment in the student ghetto. Voices and faces from the intersection of memory and thought loop, bend, and arch like ribbons of tape pulled from a VCR. A belief emerges, the way a slight twist of a kaleidoscope snaps a design into view. It can't be looked up in a book. It can't be questioned. It just is, like flesh and bones.

ANDY SMART

In Irons

We must've built ourselves a boat before I started dreaming because in the dream we're amidships in deep water under a full sail. Pressure in the atmosphere is steady.

What I know about boats I've cobbled together from movies like *Jaws*, books like *The Old Man and The Sea*, stories like Crane's "The Open Boat", and an essay by Phillip Gerard. In that last one the author emerges from a terrified huddle to find, among the aftermath of a hurricane, his candy-apple-red racer splintered and split from bow to stern. The essay ends with material loss as an indignant punctuation to the other, more profound, losses in the piece.

Sometimes I bring fear on myself. I crave it then create it in my sleep. Awake I have anxiety and I dull it with drinking. Asleep I can be a victim of consequence, circumstance, poor weather, or sailing a dreamboat into the wind. I think I love waking up screaming because I wake up. After fright there is a rush of endorphins, a great relief, glee, an asexual orgasm of *how silly I was to forget I'm just in bed*. After fright there is a blink of easiness. Then: a long fit of anxiousness, wakefulness, drunkenness, madhouse diarizing in typewriter font. In the wake of calm there is needful thinginess, a feeling that I'm an object with no value unless terror is acting upon me, that I'm like a buoy that, without a sailor to see it, ceases to exist. This is what the opposite of sleep has come to mean.

My father used to threaten me when I got sad: *I'll give you something to cry about!* Then he killed himself and made good on all that bluster. I didn't dream of him at all for months. I was afraid to.

Beyond the mountains, more mountains. Under the water, more water. I'd like to drown of heights one time.

At reliable intervals during my dream the conditions worsen. You are at the helm. This much remains constant. First the water around us begins to smell of rain and then the rain comes, attended by fog. This fog has the mouth-feel of whiskey. Soon I'm tipsy from breathing, woozy from the heave and sway. Wind is at a six on the Beaufort scale—strong breeze. Your jacket has buttoned itself and your glasses, rain-streaked, have slipped down your nose.

Dad wore thick glasses all his life. He never went out in the rain. Or if he did it was to drive me to school after his overnight shift at the Post Office, so he was half-blind with fatigue to begin with. If his lenses were smudged to blindness I never would have known.

It gets dark. Then it gets darker. Rain and wind cut sideways, jibing across the hull. They have not only taste and smell now, but color and shape: wind is a herd of blue horses and rain is a smoke-colored whip to drive them.

I never understood "The Rime of the Ancient Mariner". Never cared to. But the good south wind still blows behind and no sweet birds follow. Seagulls, ill at ease when I found us in my dream, have long since taken flight. All my book learning fails and I'm off course into what real sleep must be. Should I increase twist on the sail and power down for control? Cold now. The barometer says we're under different pressures, each of us. Mine, as the passenger, is low. Nothing, not even drowning, could be my fault. The wind in my belly should be minimal. But there's a gale in my gut and I'm sore afraid. You are a system of high pressure. You should be twirling like a waterspout, these choppy waters an invitation to turn stormy. I sense there's no bowels or appendix in you, no simple heart, no sympathetic nerves. This is not to say you're unfeeling, but that you are in tune to the music of the weather. Inside you there is rigging. Mast, mizzenmast, keel, anchor, hawse pipe. Blow the gathering gale and in the distance new music: an aeolian harp.

"Request permission to be scared," I say.

"Granted, but not advised. If you get scared you'll close your eyes. Might miss something."

My father left for work the day he died. That's what we thought, anyway, the sleeping survivors. When the gun he put in his mouth went off it must've made a noise. But no one heard it. That sleep. That fucking sleep.

Some folks tell new sailors to capsize their boats on purpose once or twice, for practice. I came to the water too late. And only because I know you. Dad upended the whole marina. Keelhauled me, put me in irons, shaved my balls with a rusty razor early in the morning.

Now lightning and big thunder. I begin to pray like I learned in grade school. Blue horses stampede across the hull again. Again.

Again. Lightning is their whinny and it is, like Dylan Thomas warned, not forked by my words.

You are smiling.

The sea sucks itself through a straw like a milkshake and sneezes before it can swallow. Waves the size of big waves surround and succeed us. We tack. We counter steer. And by we I mean you. For you this is a puzzle made of elements and you are going to solve it.

At one point we bail water. The bow is sagging. If I have nothing else I have a strong back.

I don't want to wake yet. Not yet.

We float into a meadow in the sea. A clearing. The negative space around constellations draws a portrait of the heavens plotting their revenge for crafty sailing. We drift a bit in silence. Everything disappears except the grin of the moon, the beam and tack of our boat, your unbuttoned coat, the glasses you don't wear, and me lying supine on the deck. Around you the black air paints a picture I can't see.

There begin to be stars. There have always been stars.

"You okay, Chief?" I ask.

"This," you say. "This is terrifying."

There is, you tell me, no such thing as silence. Only the sound of missing something.

So we beat on. Or whatever able-bodied seamen do in the face of the almighty.

You are my brother, brother. I start laughing and therefore I begin to awake. This is the worst- case scenario: I wake up smiling. I can fear neither day nor night nor the consequences of either for a while.

Damn the luck.

EDWARD KAITZ **Spider Sun**

SAM CHA

March 16, 2021

Fuck the killer's name, all seven syllables, two-and-a-half

generic trochees, first, middle, and last: stubby and dull

as the blade of a gas-station hunting knife. Dissolve its cheap

patternweld of history. Burn the shopworn Norman French

off the minor Old Testament prophet. Snap the Anglo-Saxon

rat-tail tang, toss the handle in the trash. Cart off the trash

to a landfill surrounded by national forests. Let it sit there,

undigested, stewing in methane and the meat juices

of a thousand thousand Big Macs. Let the last starving

timberwolf mistake it for a bone. Let it carry it off to the forest

and choke. Let the forests burn in wildfires. Let the ashes

sift into the feed trenches of factory farms,

the Pepto-Bismol muck of hog lagoons. Let the people,

unknowing, eat of the ashes of the name.

SAM CHA

The enemies address their makers and the sons their fathers

In the beginning   was the Bored

all sluggishly he moved   on the waters

blind   angelically square   chiroptero-

cherubic   tetragrammatically impaired

in *Ennui Elish*   no name for it or any all

was all that was all no between no void no

voice no light: we were all perfect once

/

oh God   tiresome one   why so

serial   so lineated   killjoy nightflitter

your   boredom water   waterboard abs

attack ad buzzkill how your commandments

drone all I want's   to give your burning bush

a Brazilian   but que   seraph   seraph

whatever angels will be will be   angels

/

You're watching I know   always   watching

planning   your next joke   your next   test

amen amen   your cold   water   Black-

water   black-   metal full-   metal   full-

volume   night-   lights   taped- lids

straitjacket how your pins   wheedle   oh

you   who   shook me   all   night

/

I'll tell all my friends   tell you   all of my friends

scabscrabble   tattertile   names you ask   anything

anything as   long as you promise   camphor me

pin me to waterboard   seal me   unhuman   re-

make me   pinniped   give me reeds   for breath

rename   my   errors   to fill   your lists

utility devil   tame terror your testament   my skin

/

And your   American   thighs   your high

and tights   your tidy   mights your

acolytes   bic lighters   Bible leaf   doom-

shouters   no   no   you shouldn't   bother

dear   I know   every   trick   each   clever

toy   black rubber   cheap shudder   deep shadow

voice gravel: how you bat, Bats, your Pop Art eyes

/

You see   the sparrow   all spectrums   fullscreen

falter   fall   but can you tell   it's me   You

who couldn't   see fire   through fennel   Your   brief

and crooked arrows   were forged by purblind   slaves

and those eyeless hawks your   predators will never

deliver my liver see   how they spread   their mourning

pinions how heedless   reel   churn   their urns of fire

/

If all the cars   glow   crawl infrared   on gray snake roads

if they are looking for   something   if they are   looking

for something to eat   if this world   is your image

they look to eat   your image   if they are   part

of the world and they   are your image   and what they

eat is your image and the world in which your images   eat

your images is your image   god   how you taste   divine

/

Like pink flamingo like ad grin all mongrel shitake

I ache gawk popeyed throat-hawked   oh lord

how your dogs do   bark   how they   spatter   I

pithy ghost   and paternoster   through evening's

last ink flamenco   pity us lord chained   to your

concrete your Platovision   unzip your Doberman

hours   stream us now   into   real   time

/

We've   met   already met   in the dark

in   between   flickering lights   last year

at Lascaux   your matchstick   game

your petty fires caveshadows your hundred

years of solitude   and Netflix   haven't you

remembered my name   so   slow   so

so slow   picky picky   long piggy

/

In the dream   you were   dead   you were

so small   father   wrapped up   in cellophane

crackle   like flowers   I forgot to bring you flowers

your feet sticking out   like two   boiled carrots   I

touched one   wrong right foot   lacquered crimson tiny

where is my father's skin   I asked   the Samedis

bloodless   how they grinned   you don't have a father

/

We were all   perfect once   then time

cut off   his father's cock   threw it

away   mindless   cock   came

falling   frothy-mouthed   and water

blushed   made   love: where we

come from   flintknife   skygash

cockcrow   brinefoam   wound

/

Whose bones are these   buried here

where lank black grass   covers   the hillock

sprouts   scratchstubble in   ochre clay

and cracked   ground mutters   rumors

near two   muddy puddles   I am not

myself today my face a ruin of my father's

face every boy's   his father's   grave

/

Who pulled   redsledded   his boy

across the frozen lake   who pinched

the tooth   pushed   pulled   who

plucked mulberries   from the high branch

greenwhite   lionspattered   who

coaxed electrons   in handtwist of copper

scrapsteel axle   to bloom in whirligig joy

/

Who cast me T-shirted out   and closed the door

on cold and tears   did you eat it   don't lie

don't you fucking lie   did I know   Eden

no   no cherry tree and axe and   sir I will not

tell a lie so I was unwarned   I had no myths

only one   father totemic vast—   how I pity

him: poor clueless daddy, younger than I am now

SAM CHA

oracles

In the year of buzzcuts
Mom and Dad gave me dinner-

money every morning.
I never ate dinner. Instead:

bought secret hipster glasses,
stashes of hairgel, a tearaway

bravado; preened wet spikes,
walked around Seoul

like I belonged there. I imagined
I was someone's shadow.

I grew skinny with movies.
In the dark, in the *bee-deh-oh*-booth—

the cathodes asked questions
of current and fluorescence.

The VCR sighed and sybilled.
From the next room

someone moaned like Cinemax.
I thought I knew the future, then:

the round spooling of it,
its generosity and malice,

the hiss of snow. How one day
everything would become real.

ZEDEKIAH SCHILD   **Parachuting in a Lion Storm**

M.J. TURNER

Haddock

We drove the fish home in an endless
Pontiac, a languid green water bug
propelling itself through half-flooded intersections,
windshield washers chiggering in the rain.
Glow worm headlights sing through the puddles.
My scabby knees sat in the backseat
beneath a paper bag; its hot oil soaks through,
pooling on my red rain slicker.
Impermeable. The fish wrap not—I smell unraveling.
Disintegrating batter, fish, French fries,
plopping noises in the dark. My grandmother sprinkling
vinegar on the upholstery over and over.

ADAM DAY

Expanse of Reality

The costume
is no less important

than the migration
through barriers –

masked faces
in the sloe-black, lit

by flashbangs,
the stream widens,

rapid, the sound
of heads like smaller

stones knocking
against each other

under shallow water.
And on the reef

the whistling buoy
bellows like a patient bull.

LAURA REECE HOGAN

Heart as Siphonophore

The researchers had imagined it, whipsawing
through silty sleeves,

the giant siphonophore, sea worm of such ghostly
fiber and length it would take hours

to watch it pass, the writhing blue bioluminescent
skin of it simultaneously here and far.

Now they witness it, photograph it, stare
at the improbable, slithering 150-foot

figment, ribboning in a quantum
state, the floating bell of head so distant

from the end of its colonized chambers
that the steadiness steers far from the fret—

stingers jostle in the eerie suck and ripple of its path.
Now, *praya dubia,* leap and swim forward

with sureness, now, wind sideways in uncertain fatigue.
The head arrives in an Australian oceanic canyon,

while the tail trails in a different time zone. So far
from true cadence of itself, two places at once:

there, the water glows aqua in your presence,
and here, the long, thin muscle still heaving,

reaching along the night-drenched bottom.

SHARON TRACEY

Driving up Haleakalā, House of the Sun

Cherry-colored trucks and pickups rust
as the sun torches a vacant
building, a field shorn of sugarcane,
a faded billboard so forlorn
it seems to say *I'm sorry*
as the car begins to climb
before we pass him—
a bronzed man carrying a six-foot white cross
on his right shoulder,
steadying it with Picasso hands
as he trudges uphill to the point
where earth, sea, and sky
form a perfect trinity.
Later, back home,
I won't mention him.
I'll talk about the humpbacks
breaching in Maalaea Bay,
my own pilgrimage
to the Merwin Palm Forest,
the hotshot surfers in Paia,
the silverswords on the summit
of the dormant volcano.
The air is thin. We breathe in
what we can breathe.
See what we choose to see.
I won't mention that clouds
conceal the pilgrim's road.

JAY BRECKER

Albuquerque, NM: January 5, 2020

—in memorium Carole Brieant

Where she was last seen

in the unhappy hour—

even the beauty of pointless palm trees

aggrieved.

We arrive via similar portals.

We depart through various exits.

A day gray clouds the sky.

Above, too vast—too open,

its corners rounded, and wild

turkeys meander back and

over the long road that drifts

forth toward the foothills and

memory. Lost in the morning

of the report; someone

props a red spirit-stick on her favorite chair.

Echoes of a friend—a dream

freighted—

an image of dried cornstalks

at the edge of the fence;

spectacle crushed under tire treads;

a stuffed animal shorn of its color by weather;

stuck in a reverie, ill-defined among tree limbs.

JAY BRECKER

Aleatory

One day, drawn on the wind,
3 coins tossed 6 times equaled
a hexagram releasing those
pigs and those fishes, foretold
by the I Ching, citing a future
of pain carved in the apse
of our bodies as you avowed,
in the village chapel, to register
and microchip my heart.
The witnesses: a witless bench;
a nameless, timid cat—better
to call than approach—lost
one day like thought; or soon
enough like me, an item omitted
from a shopping list you recall
while searching among the shelves
of unrelated ingredients.

JULIA LISELLA

I'm Receiving Now

I'm receiving now, arms bare and wide
the rain on the window, the plot without an ending

I can understand. Even now, the temperature outside to inside,
the walls a blank cream color, not a shimmer or a way to go.

I'm receiving now, all the excuses and pardons,
all the shirred edges, the unmade beds, the photographs

unidentified and yellowing, maybe my mother's friend, my father's
cousin. In the middle of a dark road the oil slicks, the cars passing

but not arriving. Who is going anywhere? I'm receiving now
the gifts left on the doorstep, no it's the mail, boxed and damp

in the cold rain. I'm receiving now my paces,
my permission. The flood at my feet is wild with its own

abundance. How silly I've been. The furniture cramped and full
of dust and blankets, the couch worn and creasing its leather face,

my hands extended. I'm receiving all the grief here it is here it is.

JENNIFER BARBER

Foothills, Memorial

I've forgotten the names
        cut into the granite

in Seyssinet-Pariset
        where the road rises

toward the plateau of Vercors
        but I remember learning

the Resistance fighters
        captured and held there

were executed facing the cliff
        in 1944, just before

the end of the Occupation.
        Our friend was silent

next to us. We'd walked
        a grassy path to get there.

We stood reading but not
        remembering the names.

JENNIFER BARBER

Holbein's "Christ Lying in the Grave"

You see into the coffin
as though a panel had been replaced
by glass. How thin he is,

a red gash beneath his ribs,
his head and his feet tinged green.

How near the coffin lid to his face.
How near the surface your own fear
of tight spaces, how hard to breathe.

You notice his hand,
dark green, and below the wrist,
a purple bruise where the nail goes in.

That he will return
to his disciples walking the road
is nowhere foretold here

unless you consider the air
lit by a hidden candle.

SARAH DECKRO — **Night Fountain**

JANE POIRIER HART

A Day

is a speck in the compound eye of a fly,
a single kernel kicked from the bird feeder.

It's a thick forest of wild-thinking
the morning your mother can't be found, when
she should be home, but isn't, and
her cats are nowhere in sight….
When you track her down at the hospital, confused
and combative, the words "inoperable brain tumor"
slung around her neck,
a day's a spiked pit disguised as a mossy bed.

A day is an inch of crocus growth in newly revealed soil,
the slow, slow siphoning of chlorophyll from summer.

A day is all you need,— you swear. Then it isn't.

JANE POIRIER HART

Fevered Is

My child self, sick, floating above couched body,
mother moving about, kitchen klicks, onion
of soup, ladle where I ache to be held.

Wet paper drinking ink,—

Minnows, shoaling, foraging for food,—

The tiny murmuration I witnessed this morning,—
starlings flying from bread to branch as one.

This is how I want to want. Single-purposed, sprung
by a fever that moves each neuron, in perfect unison,
—to you.

JONATHAN AIBEL

Disappointments

The machines weren't as interesting as I hoped;
Not like *Star Trek,* Dr. McCoy waving
a salt-shaker and quiet electronic throbs; no,
the MRI's demented alarm clock
circled your head. You got industrial strength
ear-plugs, unable to hear me, out
in the waiting, too far,
but still listening.

Fighting claustrophobia, you sang yourself
show-tunes, you told me later, *Oklahoma,*
then *Flower Drum Song.*

Meningioma we tasted the word,
argued what to say to your mother, my father,
explain to our son.

We held hands as they gave us a tour
of treatments; high energy x-rays shot
from half a giant Bell phone handset,
multi-leaf collimators hidden inside,
healing invisibly, no swirling lights,
red beams, or holographic images.

Even the Gamma Knife® is only
a frame your head fits in, with a plastic dome:
not something the Hulk would wield,
to crush the evil that hides in your skull,
among who I love
and what I do not
and am unable to say.

ROBERT WILSON

Vitrectomy

I wear blue socks with traction soles and a hospital gown. A prep nurse checks my pulse, 48, and offers a sedative. Doctor Salaam, dressed in crabapple scrubs, draws an *L* above my left eye brow with a black sharpie. An anesthesiologist, the solution to the problem of pain, uses the word *titration* before releasing fentanyl in my wrist. He takes my blood pressure repeatedly in the operating room, the cuff inhaling, exhaling around my upper arm interrupting my twilight sleep. The surgeon in the room, bright as imaginary heaven, uses a freezing probe, encircling bands, and a C3F8 bubble that floats in and out of my frightened vision for two months. Nights, I close my eye and streaks of light flash in the otherwise routine darkness. My head positioned parallel to the ground for a week, I walk Diebold Road, a morning glory vine twisting itself up the U-channel steel sign post, the *B* peeled off Diebold. Morning glories dilate at dawn, water filling their veins. Newborns can be born with morning glory syndrome, myriad blood vessels curving from the optic disc like petals from a stigma. I squint at their curvy sentences as if learning to read flower. The Aztecs used morning glory seeds to visit the divine. They called the flower *bones of children* and *coats of heaven*. Human retinas, the wallpaper of our brains, are the thickness of a human hair. My C3F8 bubble started out the size of the earth, although unlike the earth, it never really hurt. Sometimes when we are young a particle lodges in our eye and we have to ask for help to have it removed.

JW SUMMERISLE

bodkins

pierce & poke   astride
a needle known by earth
& isaac newton knows
its hurts   his bones   his
bagged up flesh   sac
of bones and teeth   he
perceives its colours   unwinds
its shapes and dog rose
rose berries rose hips
and thorns he is
sick   he is struck
in his organ   soft &
pink & orange
scrambled white in the
crowns of taller trees
he pokes   he finds
in piercings   pores
sore flesh   sore hurt
his eyes held wide
in a spectrum
of sour sharpened fruit

Note: (Isaac Newton experimented with light & vision by jamming a bodkin needle into his eye socket)

JW SUMMERISLE

unremarkably arboretum

window-climbing boys
moulder, mid-ring faerie
dance & maudlin. i would

make a love of thick
leaves & thin grass, sand
turned water when upright
and cast unfavourably in

cloud but but disrupted

dim mushroom cups dampen
above a length of grass
grown enough for loss.

gravity likes its light like small
girls given a little air.

JW SUMMERISLE

hordeum vulgare

it's always this house   it's
a feature of the language

grass stalks of hair build
lengths of sky & the
outer layer is called
bran   trace minerals

orchestrate   placing fibres
in the mouth of god
and praying with players

of thin reeds rasping
for sanctuary   for
safe space   o

mother   mother   the
long grass   it grows
whiter than the sky

JASON MONTGOMERY — **Imperial Rattler**

GLORIA MONAGHAN

Cormorant on the Strand

The crew had code words for me when on set.
Bad was Georgia.
Very bad was Florida.
The worst was Zanzibar.
You have to wonder about Zanzibar
and what it entailed
beyond speech, beyond body, the word itself.

A region of Tanzania, black coast,
a central Swahili trading town.
An unsettled place, a possession of Portugal,
and notorious Arab slave trader
Tippu Tip, who traded ivory and clove,
died in Stone Town in 1905.
Can you imagine being named after gunfire?

Eventually free
and blended into obscurity
a mix of
Arab, Bantu, Persian, and Indian.

After each overthrow, it appeared
to be independent of any country
a land unto itself
a direct rule, as it were.

When I was Georgia,
it was a given that anything
could happen; a light overturned,
a fall brought on by a combination of
Nembutal, Seconal, candy bourbon juice
lewd-monkey-throwing-food-at-a-party kind of Georgia.

What does it mean to be Georgia?
To be good again,

like when you are young and brush your teeth
before going to Mass.

The sun goes down in three layers:
gray-blue, dusk
a line of fire-orange, followed by a trail of purple.
You have some time to think.

In Florida I was picking food out of a dumpster,
soliciting grocery boys.
I'd been knifed in Los Angeles.

(I knew then I'd been knifed)

In a certain month of summer Florida
the water temperature may exceed the air.
Parasites develop near the shoreline;
be aware not to tread so close to the shoreline,
be caustic but supreme when dealing with candy boys,
note shadows after five. Don't play cards with Kevin
until you've had a few more.

When in Zanzibar, all bets are off.
I once walked on the roof
of my New York brownstone
at the edge when I was in Zanzibar.

Zanzibar with its turtles,
thieves, skeletons, blue
water, and vast sand.

Be in their flowing cups freshly rememb'red.
This story shall the good man teach his son....*

Lorenzo asked why.
Larry, why do women fall in love with men?
In the summer, halved mussel shells scatter the beach
blue-silver outlined purple.

Zanzibar is not a place;
it is a location of the mind.
Ungovernable country,
a place in the sun
outlawed wilderness of wolves and women
dancing in the desert in Fellini's 8½
tranced-out women of Dionysus
all the more sexual in their decline;
of course, it's the pubescent boys who dance
with her—eyes rolling in and out of her
head into the earth, sky divine.

* From William Shakespeare's Henry V, Act IV, Scene iii

GLORIA MONAGHAN

Remnants of my Property

Hey, old man.

Hi.

I didn't know then that he was recording our conversations.
Every day I called my brother until the last picture
Freud.

I really should have won the Academy Award
for that picture.

My brother worked for the CIA,
a kind of recordkeeper.

My lines in *The Heiress*
spell it out; *I'm not a mercenary.*

After the accident, I had to navigate things
differently, use my face in ways I never realized
I could; my hands, my walk,
as if some wild thing caught hold of me from the
inside—

I could not let anyone see
what I knew about my body.
I'm not a mercenary.

In *Suddenly, Last Summer,* I come to heal
Catherine in the aftermath of Saint Sebastian,
poet, lover, destroyer, fraud. Instead I became him.

Some horrible things were said on that set.
Katharine Hepburn spit in the director's face.
She did that for me;

can you imagine?

You are beneath contempt.

I remember it well, being beneath contempt.

I'm not a mercenary; I have
remnants of my property.

GLORIA MONAGHAN

A Place in the Sun

The best picture of Monty and Elizabeth Taylor
was on the set of *A Place in the Sun.*
He is 30, she is 17
part of a black-and-white studio series.
Their bodies engrave each other.

His hand squeezes her bicep,
she is laughing.
He has a cigarette in his mouth
managing a dazzling smile,
broad tweed jacket open white collar;

born for the screen and high-resolution photos,
she looks directly at the camera,
he, away to some guy dragging equipment.
Her body relaxed, pops
above beyond,

his hand in his pocket.
He calls her Bessie the Cow
at the premiere. Later,

after the accident, she stays with him,
puts her salary down for him
to star next to her in *Reflections
in a Golden Eye.*

In this photo there is glamour, the adobe wall of the studio,
the fake street, or intended alley
a moment stopped in time
immortalized lines
of his cheek, white teeth, and cigarette.

He carries her upside down
over his shoulder,
her broad backside an autumn bell;
maybe it was a green A-framed skirt.
A saint in the street.

Judas in the waiting room.
There is always someone
who understands you without words
a glance, a smile, a tear,
who cradles your head in their hands
saves you from the wreckage.
It is what some call
a haven of mercy,
the body is a home for the soul
we return to broken and bruised, cracked and lovely.

GLORIA MONAGHAN

Raintree County

She may have seen him for what he was—
artist, saint, deplorable, genius.
He may have seen her for the same;
beauty, drug-addled, violet-eyed.

She sat there doing her hair,
simple white tight-fitting sweater, black pants.

He, black suit, white loosened collar, loose black tie,
black spectacles at the edge of his nose.

Cautioning his Bessie, *there is something I need to remind you about,*
was she shushing him, or were they just talking or gossiping?

There was no advice he could really give her other than

be yourself.

I will be myself,
I will need to rewrite some of these lines.
I will need something more to respond to than this ...
You know what I mean, Bessie.

There are no staged photos
of open hands on his knees.

DAVID DODD LEE — **A Hateful Mob**

NEIL SILBERBLATT

Elegy for the Man of Steel

As a child, I watched
George Reeves darting into and out of phone booths
to change his clothes -
tearing off his fedora and horn-rimmed glasses,
stripping off his suit, white button down shirt and tie -
revealing cape and tights
which, like him, were always at the ready.

I watched him racing and flying
across our small black & white TV set
to fight untruth, injustice and the un-American way
and wondered where he stood
on the beatings of white Freedom Riders
or the hosings of black protestors
who also raced ——
in torn and water-soaked suits and ties -
across our TV set.

The summer of my sixth year -
when the twisted black & white bodies of
Schwerner, Chaney and Goodman
were found in Philadelphia, Mississippi -
I questioned what side Clark or his alter ego
were on, and whether
he had arrived there
too late, even with all that racing and flying.

Surely, he was on their side.
He, an outside agitator
and a New York City journalist.

Then, after all those phone booths,
all that racing and flying,
George got himself shot and killed
in his mid 40s —
like our other heroes.
So, of course,
he was one of us.
I knew it all along
and loved him all the more.

JENNA LE **My Happiest Times Have Been in Asian Restaurants**

LIBBY MAXEY

Okuribi

The hills around Kyoto burn tonight
to guide the wandering dead home, carefully.
Each bonfire brushstroke is a path, the light
a boat, a gate, a word's wide effigy.
The monks who pledge to walk a thousand days
among those trees, beads clicking midnight prayer
at every sacred stone, put on the grave's
white linen and a funeral purse, prepared
for failure with a blade. A tarrying
and less ambitious traveler, I accrete
the bold suggestion as it blurs again
to dark, and crowds unfold onto the streets
that have themselves known fire. We go our ways
and hope to find them bright in ash as blaze.

LIBBY MAXEY

Not Brought up for Waka

Kanoya Airbase Museum

kamikaze poems

say   no time for pillow words

one wrote simply   death

like the iron kettle poured

at Rabaul   do what's done

LIBBY MAXEY

A New Old Saying

It may be we are like the chickadee—
Our set of songs and calls expressive but
Familiar, collocations standard cut:
A few clean notes to show our quality
A gutsy cluck to buff our narrow rut.

The indignant ruffle seems our own, and is,
And so the high, thin shims of our alarm;
But given, too, as filaments that warm
A skin. Our words are the appurtenances
Of our kind—utility and charm.

Then let us not suppose that ours may be
The most important, conjuring the most
Important things. Each utterance a ghost
Of millions, each *bon mot* a surety—
We keep on whistling on a weathered post.

CHRISTIE PAGE **Bug 2**

CARLA DRYSDALE

Before the Divorce

You held on tight with both hands
as it whirled in a wide circle:
an albatross stirring the sky's
bright mind, that bowl of silence.

You held on, smiling. Purple fists
gripped its long legs
as it wound around, its radius
majestic, as though flying of its
own accord. We cheered you on.

I watched and marveled until,
from my mouth, a warning –
Let it go! When it dove, I saw
first the shadow on the sea's
tinfoil surface

the beak's blunt spear
just missed our child who sat
near you. I woke before I knew
whether or not you let go.

FRANCES DONOVAN

What a Mess I've Made

in the voice of my mother

What a mess I've made, fever makes it clear—
the socks in the dishwasher,
the bills due last Tuesday propped
against the china in the hutch.

I see the mess but not the way
to order which my daughter
always seemed to know, she could set
a great pile of clutter to rights in an afternoon.

Holidays she would chase me
from the kitchen, a paring knife in her hand,
half an onion chopped on the board
and I knew, I knew the terrible burden

I had placed on her. How she'd closed up
like an iris in late frost.

ERIC ROY

All My Wins Are Going to Need Asterisks

Blue Adderall, green tea. Granulated sugar.
Morning claps its lid against the bin of day.

At work at home, a desk or makeshift office
in a breakfast tray. Outside, you hear someone

sing *Climb Every Mountain*, low & lilting,
out of key. Down through the open window,

you see a figure in the early indigo, hooded
sweatshirt for a habit, holding the thin line

of a leash as the terrier at the end of it shudders
dots of broken excrement out onto the sidewalk.

Together they trot home, forsaking the ellipsis.
But it's the stranger who seems lighter, relieved,

unencumbered & *familiar*. Yes, far less strange
than, say, father, brother, friend, or even yourself

still in the act of imagining facts are not okay
as daylight arrives narrowing its eyes, cheated

by the results of winter trees, branches divulging
their single-elimination bracket for fallen leaves.

JENNIFER MARTELLI

Fascism

So now I have Venmo and no use for credit cards. I can't even chop

my sadness into powder on the long edge of debt. I lost the milk glass

cake dish, the one with a fluted stand, the one shaped like a little woman

with a big brim hat. I can't draw out my sadness on its surface. I don't

even carry bills to roll into a straw. I don't own straws. I shave with a cartridge—

no straight-edge razor to slit an eye-hole and pull a red satin dress through—

all empire-waisted and bell-sleeved. My daughter dances on Instagram:

her red silk camisole, her velvet wine leggings make her a single intention,

a thick lip-sticked mouth moving through her tiny Park Slope apartment.

She dangles mirrors from her ceiling to make it bigger, balances bowls

of water on her bed table, her bureau drawer, the back of a lavender book

to capture more light than she'll ever need. She films through a prism,

her iPhone on a tripod, moves to Liz Phair, Björk on Spotify: songs sung

before she was born. She says that I still shave my legs smooth because of fascism.

You don't even know how bad it's pulled you to the right and then she laughs.

WILLY CONLEY **Time Expired**

WILLY CONLEY **Dual Latches**

ERWIN PONCE

Binibini

— beginning with a line from Bill Knott

Sunny or storm the clouds always once

mean their meaning without meaning to

leave what they meant where they meant to.

I am surrounded by several types of women

women haunted themselves by other women

eyes drawn in/to their mothers' mirrors.

Rain is mud now and puddles of water

now ocean now lake now river back to breath

black stones sunk in cups of water.

The city and the whole sin/grace thing

is full of meaning to me always meaning

different people to the same thing.

MID WALSH

On the Commuter Boat

Even the moon this night
can't sleep on the harbor.
The waves are too busy fighting
to give back light.

I try to still myself, but
my reflection wakes
past the bluff, between
the blank sky and restless waves.

I think it must be utterly still
between the stars. No wind;
no water churning, only
the miracle of nothing-there.

And I imagine quiet
inside, beneath
the stressful turn and spit of waves.

There, the light is not visible;
a tender anemone lies
lovingly cupped in the cleft of a rock;

a warm spring in the water's floor,
lips forever pursed, whistles
so low you can almost hear

crystals of life pluming
toward clear air.

JENNIFER L. FREED

Surface

Only later, when you finally let me hear

an occasional gasp

for breath

do I begin

        to see

how long

you have barely been holding your head above

the waves

all the while smiling,

as though your legs were not thrashing

below.

JENNIFER L. FREED

As in a Window Glass

And then, a week later, a shift
of weather and I would see it all
differently.

Again and again like this,
as in a window glass—reflections,
refractions. A face emerging, yours, but
layered under sway of light.

At first, I didn't notice shadow.
I didn't know to look.
I reached out, a siren wailed, the wind
shimmered sun through trees.

Again and again, I thought I'd seen you,
but I know now
that I didn't know how
to make sense of this
ripple of movement, that
flash of blue
in the corner.

ANNE ELEZABETH PLUTO

St. Francis Meets Mary Kay
at the Prairie Pink Barbie Dream House

The Virgin doesn't live here
but her animals do the donkey
She rode into Bethlehem – the sheep
that surrounded the manger – the cattle
that brought her warmth during
labor without a midwife
or her mother – St. Anne – her bewildered husband
betrothed to a pregnant girl who walked
with a circle of stars at her feet desiring pomegranates
and charming the snakes in Nazareth. St. Francis
has come here to the Texas heat – his tonsured
statue – always holding that Girl's son in his arms
the animals they come in pairs and kick up
dust the pink house as tight as sex
as a womb ready to burst.
Its blood and bones alive and trembling.

ANNE ELEZABETH PLUTO

Circle of Stars

The yellow church and onion domes recall
the turbaned severed heads of the last
Kazan Tatars –Victory at Astrakhan ornate as blood itself
in Moscow – every Red Square picture postcard parade
marches past St. Basil's 4500 miles and the summer
apart the yellow church is closed
the young priest
quizzes my baptism – I cannot recall the name
but the copper dome rises above the Brooklyn Queens
Expressway the Transfiguration – the Annunciation
the Dormition of the beautiful Mary
say her name and she will
open the oak doors and step
in red and green in gold gently
between her circle of stars
Come in
Come in
Come in and light your candle
Come in
And I will
Handle him.

ANNE ELEZABETH PLUTO

Sandy Texas Candy House

Where the gingerbread tastes
like baked afternoon sun and
Mary walks the rooms silent
as a nun the sun pours through
the pink curtain sheet there's a tear
in the eye of the virgin – a smudge
in the fuchsia lipstick she wore
to her first prom – all the sad
hot years later she made
him cover the glider to a match
lit to remembrance – a saint's candle
purchased at the flea market
on Clovis – inside - where they
still sell Coca Cola in green glass
bottles from Old Mexico where
she wanders and watches the Lady
who sells parakeets – neatly lined up
in their happy cages – singing
and she wonders why that doesn't
happen in the sandy Texas
Candy House.

ANNE ELEZABETH PLUTO

We Started Out as Liars

For MKS

You were a gentile
My family were Poles.

You were a Jew
And we are Russians

For the most part.
It is only a story

You tell to survive
A fiction that follows.

A chapter.
A mystery.

A test.
Then it is over.

And we rest.
We rest.

MEGGIE ROYER

Noah Leaves the Ark

Magic tells us that one out of every twelve people

will eventually dream of a doorless world.

That windows, if locked, will become shattered.

That cellars, if trapped, will become unhandled.

I remember, once, as you passed through one door

and I through another,

how we spent years doing this

until we realized our hands

had never touched the same knob.

It's not with grief that love ends,

but with understanding,

like an animal finally rising from slumber,

or the myth that woman

was pulled from man's rib.

The amygdala learns how to re-wire.

The limbic system just a system,

and sleeping alone

is almost a kind of giving.

K. T. LANDON

This Is Not the End of the World

but this is how it ends:
the too-slow
realization. The long wait
for what has happened
to happen
to us.
How kind we are
without touching.
How we keep
working shopping going
as if effort counts
towards our final grade.
He tells me
I'm beautiful
all the time and
all the time I am
afraid. Lions sleep on
the pavement, goats
push a merry-go-round—
the world already
moving on. Beyond
the window I see
every last bird.

STEPHEN NELSON

pages from **Asemic Tantra**

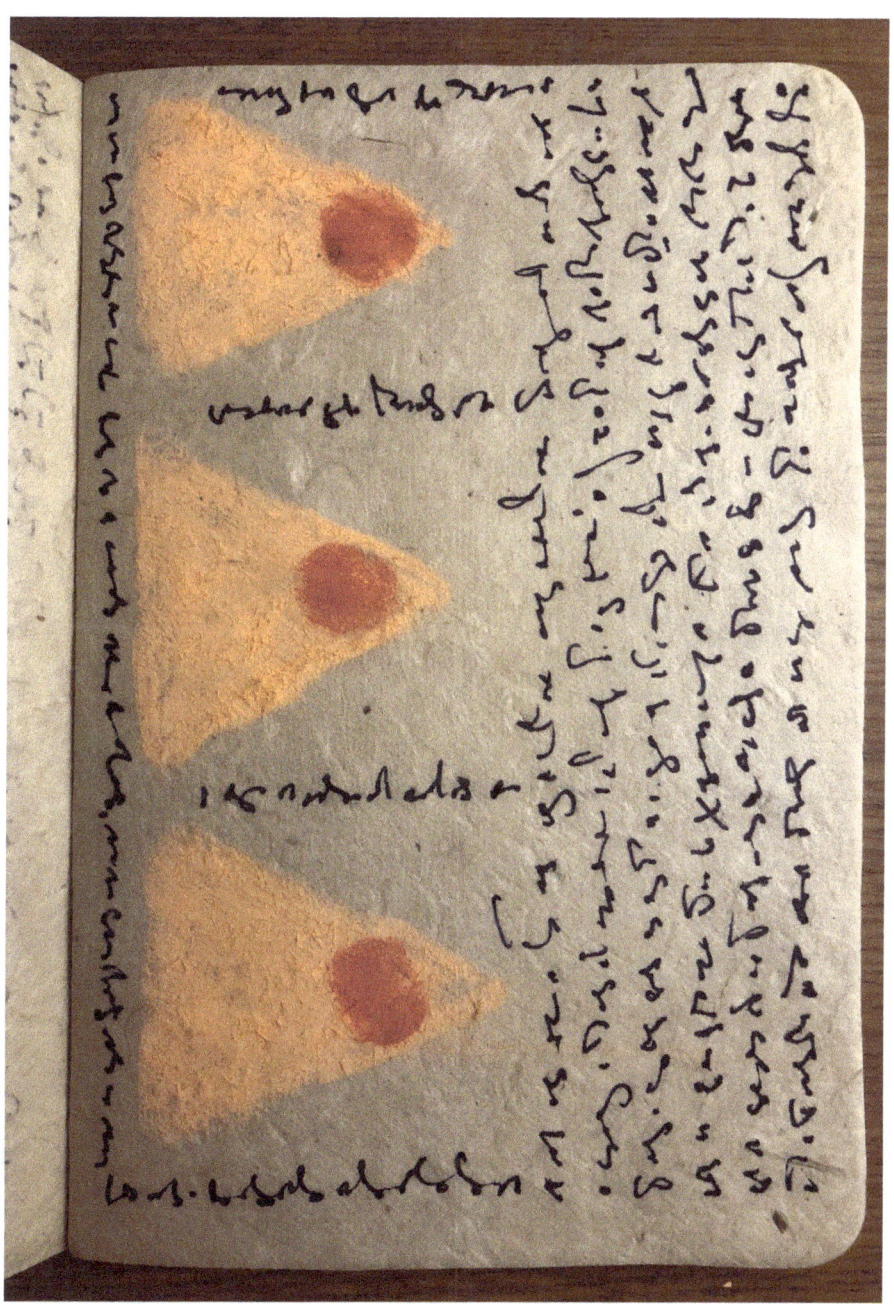

119

STEPHEN NELSON

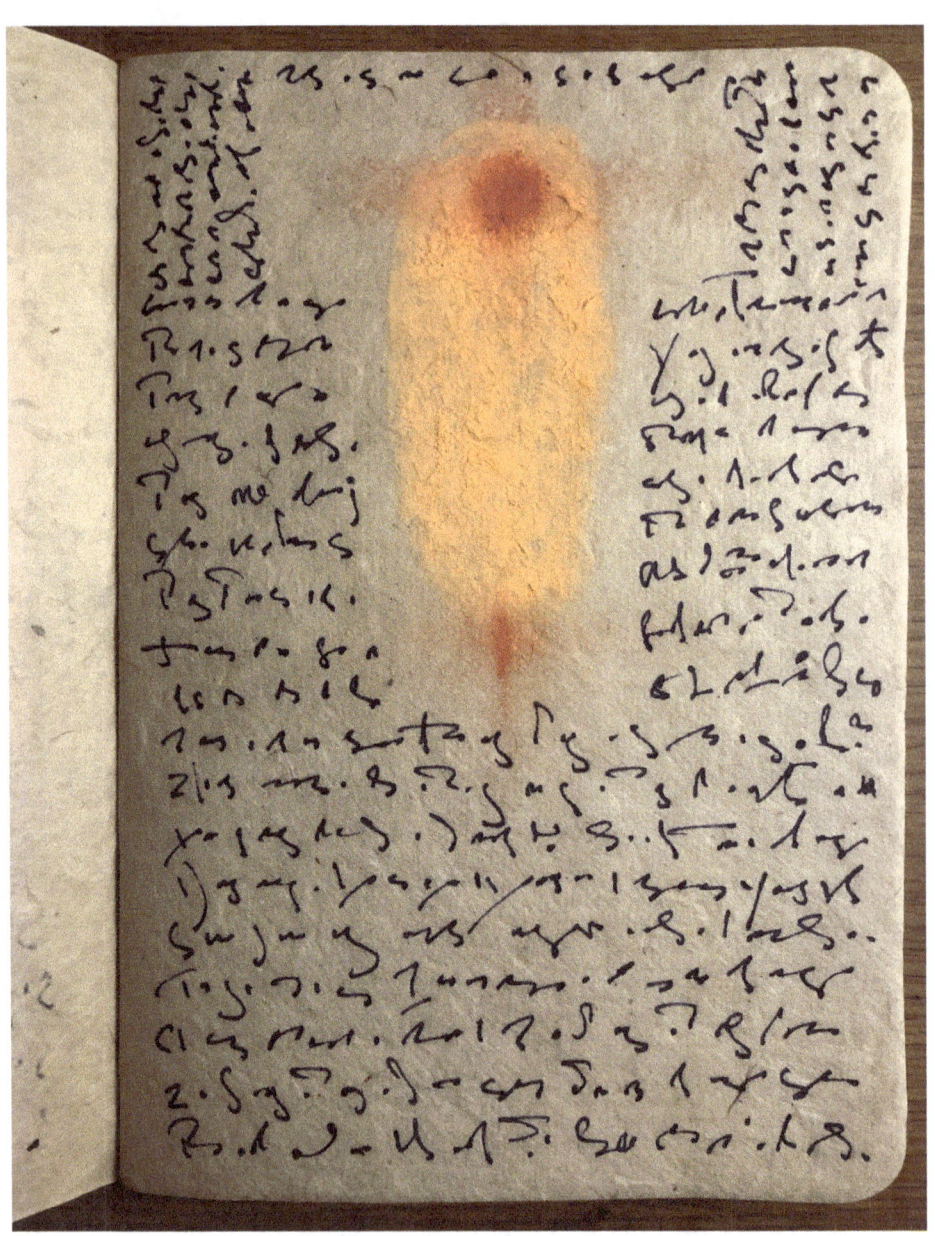

pages from **Asemic Tantra**

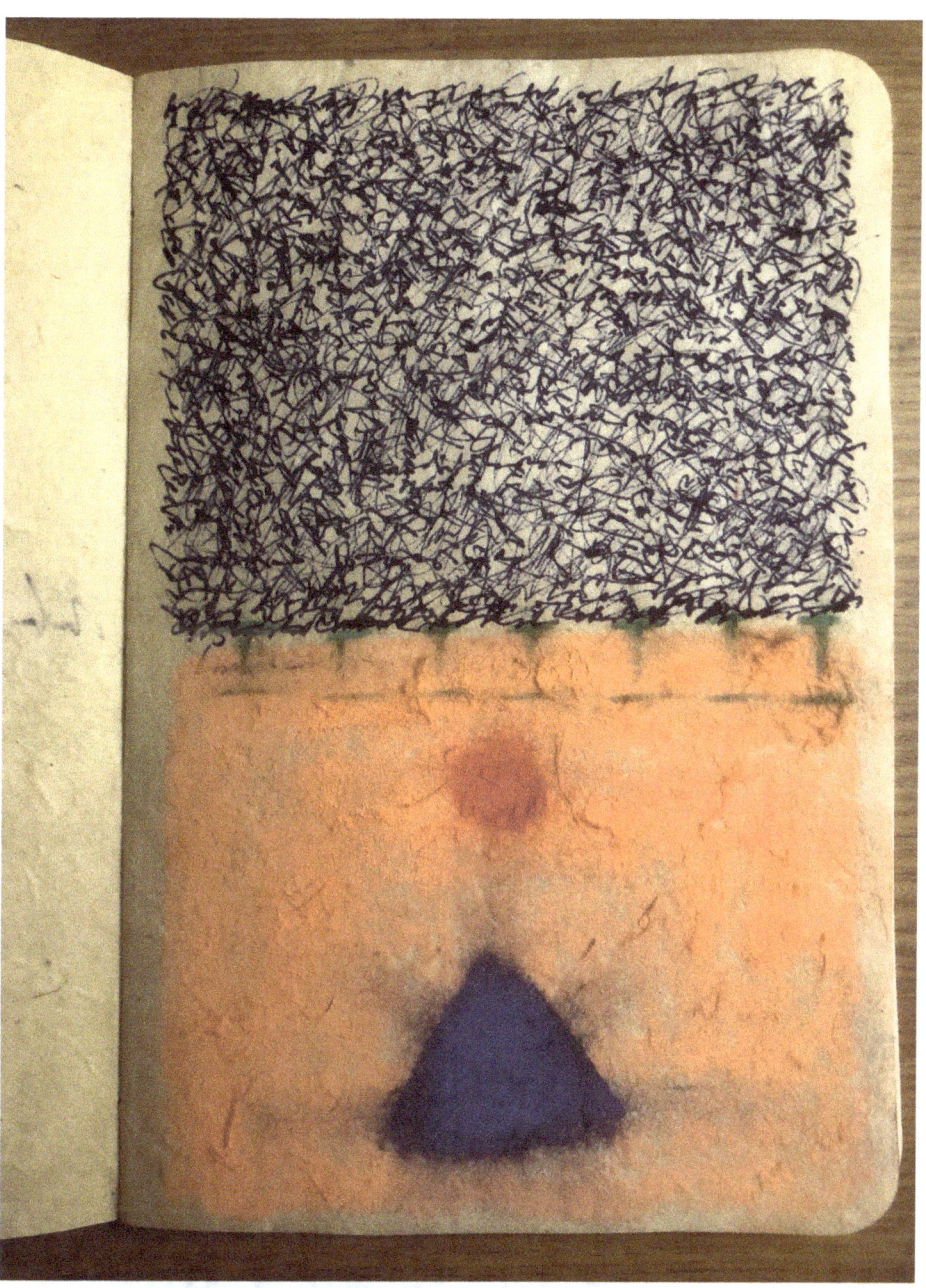

STEPHEN NELSON   pages from **Asemic Tantra**

HEATHER NELSON

Review: *Petition* by Joyce Peseroff
Carnegie Mellon University Press, 2020.

Joyce Peseroff's intimate, thoughtful and well crafted book of poems, *Petition* got more unsettling, in the best way poetry can, each time I sat down with it. The book sat on my dining room table for over a month, reminding me that poetry is food, to consume small portions often, but slowly. Before opening the book, I would glance at the bird on its cover, wondering what type it was, resolving to look it up, or to ask one of my ornithologically inclined buddies. It was only this morning, the identity of the bird still undetermined, that I noticed the bird's background. It isn't sitting in a nest, as I assumed, or in a gutter pipe, as I've seen before. It is sitting in the mouth of a cannon.

The subtle seriousness of the cover art, and the book's title, are clues that the book's scope will be broad, that its intent is to make the reader examine her world very closely. The book moves between global and local concerns, between political and personal perspectives, deftly and links them in ways that are lyrical and compelling. The book's title poem, "Petition" has some of the solemn ceremonial tone of a land acknowledgement, some of the accessible advocacy of a MoveOn.Org email. It slowly pounds a drum beat of demands, but the rhythm doesn't escalate, it pauses, meanders, gives you a half smile, meets your eye. The poem is earnest in its wants, but rueful about its reach, wryly acknowledging the role of the petitioner in contributing to the grievance. The poem leaves room for whimsy "maybe they'll mill the stocks for bookends" and while serious about the harm our world has suffered, is skeptical about the prospects for redemption " give us eternity again, we'll set things right."

In "Petition" the poet pleads on our behalf for "time to restore the forests and the sea." In the poem "Missing Hiker Kept Journal of Her Ordeal", the forest asserts itself, upending the hiker's expectation of a journey she could control, through familiar territory, on "our land." The poem's title is drawn from a Boston Globe headline in May 2016, and is in part the story of a tragic accident, of how a peaceful encounter with a beautiful natural setting went wrong. However, while the title leads the reader to believe the poem might be a journal entry, the story of one woman's suffering, it is more of a textual evidence log, containing scraps of information which form a jagged picture of the often unacknowledged power dynamics in our relationship with nature. As the hiker gets out of range of human contact, her sense of control, her attempts at connection, and even her identity disintegrate. The poem's repetition effectively marks her desperation, the hikers' texts are "undelivered" and "never received", read only too late and far away "on a Navy training base." The poem starts with the immediacy of the I, we are walking with the hiker in real time. By the second day the I becomes more existential "I kept searching." In short order, the hiker becomes a "she", the wardens called "her name" and we " know she knew she was dying ." The agency of the poem moves away from the hiker and leaves her dilemmas with the reader. The most poignant and pressing question the poem poses is "[c]an I understand the pain of others only by suffering, which I hate?" This question reminded me that there are people sleeping and freezing in my city, their calls unheard and unheeded, and that the hiker's personal tragedy is also a collective tragedy. Nonetheless, personal suffering is intimate and can make us selfish "is suffering a thicket with a bird inside, every other singer competition for a mate?" The poem closes with an image that is clearly tragic, but personal and impersonal at the same time. The "photo of items placed outside the tent" are markers both of one woman's death and the detritus of human suffering all around us.

The poet makes it clear that it's just as easy to get lost in the city as in the woods. The poem "Lonely in Japan" paints a beautiful ("the clouds go plum") but painful picture both of a traveller's isolation and of the loneliness and disconnection of many city dwellers. The poem's speaker is a traveller to Japan who introduces us to her dilemma by remarking that "[i]n Japan you can hire a family if your wife has died and your daughter won't speak to you." While the fracturing of tight and sometimes limiting social bonds is an issue impacting modern Japanese families, the atomization of society and the automation of intimacy are problems we all face. "[T]he blue face of the TV" is now the blue face of the iPhone screen, we are all watching others and wanting to be noticed. Peseroff's images of women who raise and lower their shades daily in tandem are vivid, and the expectation of the lonely neighbors that this mutual gesture will be recognized, that our neighbor " will notice the day it stays down" pulls a powerful punch. Written from the perspective of a visitor to a "foreign capital " "a city in which your visa has expired", the poem is highly effective in driving home its message that wherever you are, "loneliness stays the same."

While isolation and disconnection weave their way throughout *Petition*, the book is also full of humor and insights into the power of writing to create meaning from the unexpected experiences we wouldn't choose but have to live with. The poem "Sonnet on the Solstice" defied my expectations and opened my eyes. I was looking for a poem about summer, but found one about winter, or summer's heat invading winter. I was looking for a poem with conventional rhyme a but instead, the rhymes are hidden in the lines, with wonderful enjambment, "Overwhelmed by love's bright light, who sees/a thing? My loves, I couldn't bear the dark/without your veined and noisy black lace wings." Instead of being about literal murder, this sonnet conveys the rage of a writer who battling with herself about her art, angry at her inability to kill her darlings, she can only "picture them dead." The poem is full of wordplay that keeps the reader on her toes:"shoots" not from a gun, but from tulips. Transformative verbs "the sun hunkers" and "the fly a grackle on my nerves" show the slow and difficult process of crafting the poem. In the end, the poem is an ode to the flies who are her muse and companions and the poet is mother to her work now that the "twentysomething" is only home on occasion or not at all.

Another vision of motherhood emerges in "Turkeys in Twilight", the book's penultimate poem. The poem's turkeys are "moms with half-/grown poults." The poem is full of dark humor and allusion-Edward Gorey, comic imagery of windows marching in their weeds, raucous rhyme of moms and Toms. It is also somber, these mothers are not only minding their poults, they are our watchers too. The poem reads as a comment on colonial settlement, our country's native birds are turning their dignified backs on the gabbling imports, chickens. They'll reclaim conservation land and turn it feral again, quietly without pomp and not in response to our petitions.

Petition's last poem "Irish Music", leaves us not with the land, but with each other, in our fallen state, for comfort. The poem's three line stanzas blend the intimate perspectives of abstracted people- a blind man with sight restored and a woman with Alzheimer's. The disorienting return of color and shape to man's world "he walks in a painting by Klee or Miro" is vividly rendered as is the visceral panic that can accompany Alzheimer's "a dark red rug/looks like a hole in the floor _/a bloody hole." While the world is not restored, there is some restoration in this poem, restoration of the man's sight, which could also be insight, about what's most important. In the poem's final line the man can "hold her hand as long as it needs to be held" and this poem, and ultimately this collection, urges the reader to reach out for comfort, and to take it when it comes.

ANDY SMART

Review: Stephen Kuusisto's *Old Horse, What Is to be Done?*   Tiger Bark Press, (2020)

> One way we praise a work of art is to say it has 'vision,' and good poetry and good seeing go together almost always.
> —Jane Hirshfield, *Ten Windows: How Great Poems Transform the World*

> Boyhood:
> Blind with puppets and homemade songs . . .
> It was sweet to be lost with the crickets.
> —Stephen Kuusisto, *Remembering Donald Justice*

It's an old preconception about writers that, as we create, we envision an ideal reader—that peculiar and particular audience who is the exact match for our work. Often, writers are said to imagine this shadowy figure leering over their shoulder as the words hit the page. If the ghost is felt nodding in approval we carry on; if it clears its throat or perhaps folds its arms, we are interrupted, thwarted. But what if we forgo the distance between writer and perfect reader? That is exactly what Stephen Kuusisto does in his latest book *Old Horse, What Is to be Done?*

Kussisto's newest collection is, among other things, a love song to his muses. His ideal readers are the retinue of poets who inspire him, the spirits of places where he has felt most alive, the empty tea cups which dance after the metaphorical housekeeper has toddled off to bed. In *Old Horse, What Is to be Done?* there are nods to Robert Bly, Tomas Transtromer, Doug Anderson, Apollinaire, Mozart, Ted Berrigan, James Tate, Meg Kearney, Jarkko Laine, Andy Warhol, and others.

We who are present for this book's arrival in the here-and-now are simply lucky recipients of Kussisto's gleeful celebration of his craft. We're in the right place and the right time.

Throughout this collection, Kussisto proves—repeatedly—that it is good to be alive. This is not to say *Old Horse, What is to Be Done?* is a book with blinders on. Far from it. Consider this, from "Ode": "My nation's history is a dark river. /

If I am one of the saved, still swimming . . . / I do not want to be ashamed of the shore."

The poet neither waxes nostalgic nor despondent. Rather, he presents a poetic fact. He uses the crystalline vision Hirshfield attributes to all great poets and poems and, with his singular acuity, positions himself and his readers within the larger history of this world. In fact, the poem reads, to this reviewer, as extraordinarily mindful. The shore Kuusisto's speaker is afraid of being ashamed of is the one he's swimming toward; the poem seems, then, to call us to action. To be alive in such a way that the future is a thing to take joy in.

For the poet to invest such responsibility in his art is for him likewise to invest it with hope—such a necessary thing in these times.

Kuusisto is forever inquisitive about the role of poetry. While he stops far short of declaring an answer, he seems to hint at one: it's the poet's job to witness the state of humanity. From "Praxis: Deliberate Beauty":

> Language is a trick. God knows . . .
> art can help you live, but the atelier may smell like a water closet . . .
> Oh, but how the words stink . . .
> I wanted to be useful so I wrote a poem.
> It was not beautiful but terribly alive."

And yet, for his unflinching eye trained on the way things are, Kussisto's work is rarely, if ever, cynical. From the same poem:

"Though there are many answers to the puzzle one may call 'how to live and what to do' in the end the only solution to fear (whether your life involves disability or something else) is love."

And from "Notes on Christmas Morning," L Thoughts and poems circulate. / I love the Jesus who lets me stay blind."

Metaphor lives rent-free in *Old Horse, What Is to be Done?* but only insofar as it is allowed to by the literal. Which is to say: there's really an old horse and Steve Kuusisto talks to him. His name is Luigi and he's a retired racehorse. He lives with the poet and his wife in New York state.

That kind of grounding is emblematic of the poems in Kuusisto's new book: they wind out into some weird spaces (a Helsinki tavern where the poet is confused for a Jew, for instance) and indulge or demand serious speculation. But they always return home to earth, to the shore of which, it seems, the poet is not ashamed.

Steve Kuusisto is a blind man with acerbic wit and no compunction whatsoever about fearless observation. He is also a tender man who weeps at the sound of Enrico Caruso's tenor. That he is a poet working today is good medicine for those who love poetry with a spirit hellbent on survival. *Old Horse, What Is to be Done?* is a beautiful book. If it wasn't, it would still be terribly alive. Read it immediately.

LISA J. SULLIVAN

Review: *The Dandelion Speaks of Survival* by Quintin Collins
(Cherry Hill Publishing, 2021)

It is difficult to pass by cover art as evocative and alluring as that appearing on Quintin Collins' debut poetry collection, *The Dandelion Speaks of Survival*. Indeed, the explosive beauty of the content reflects that of the cover. A finalist for the prestigious Alice James Award, this dazzling collection begins with poems of adolescent struggles, joys, and mischief in an urban landscape and transitions to adulthood poems that confront racism and praise his family, Blackness, and of course–"Hot Flamins."

The haunting, opening poem "The Water I Came From" compels us to read on with its effective use of anaphora that cements the poem's urgent tone and a last line that pounds its historical, brutal truth into the world. The book is thereafter divided into two sections.

In section I, Collins takes us on a nostalgic, coming-of-age ride down the Chicago area's "Ravisloe Terrace." The vehicles we ride in are sometimes a Caprice Classic, sometimes an Impala, but always, Collins' vehicle—his authentic, hip poetic voice. Interestingly, the point of view in section I is second person, which creates a careful distance between the speaker and character. This allows the poet to more fully explore the emotions of the vulnerable, younger character without slipping into sentimentality.

Section I will satisfy even the most discerning poetry craft enthusiast. For example, witness the plethora of playful imagery and figurative language, including metaphor, personification, chremamorphism, and simile, in "Ice Cream Economics":

> You chase melody. Xylophone reverberations
> crawl up Ravisloe Terrace. Sneakers percuss
> sidewalks. Pause Double Dutch
> hi hats, basketball timpanis. Screen
> doors slap like cymbals...

…..

> Adolescents
> drumroll right up to the window.

Among Collins' most masterfully employed craft elements are sound devices, as seen in these fresh, rhythmic lines from "Requiem for a Freestyle":

> Lunchroom lyricists battle rap, boys who rattle back /
> impromptu lexicons, drop lessons on / finesse and flow. Blow
> after blow / slinging punchlines / they punt rhymes / to put
> the opposition on the bench. Listen to the salt they pinch /

Of note in this book are the various formatting techniques used by Collins. Page to page, nearly every poem's structure is different, from block style to tercets, columns, couplets, and breathy white space constructs (e.g., "Boys and Their Breaking") that excite the eye and complement the content.

In Section II, Collins switches to the first-person point of view allowing a more intimate, mature, confident speaker. His ability to transport the reader so fully into his urban American landscape rivals that of even Sandburg, as evidenced in this excerpt from "Why I Just Say I'm From Chicago,"

> Ask me where I'm from, and I'll tell you Metra trains
> ripple through detached home corridors into downtown Chicago,
> that fistful of potholes, soiled napkins, taxi cabs, the bucket boy
> who beats a pulse. A peripheral whisper—that's where
> I'm from the edge where deer herds dip into protected forests.

or here, in "This Is Where You Belong":

> Where the Sears Tower casts a shadow across the land,
> this is twenty-five miles southwest of Chicago. A wheat field cleared
> for a billboard that announces an outlet mall that never broke
> ground.
>
> ......
>
>   & this is Atkin Park, where a sock-swaddled padlock swung
> an eviction notice to an eye. Blood speckled hopscotch squares.

We are also introduced to Collins' brilliant "Speaks" poems in section II, the titles of which may nod to Langston Hughes. One of the most accomplished of these is the title poem "The Dandelion Speaks of Survival." Although the theme may hold respectful glints of Maya Angelou's "Still I Rise," this poem carries Collins' original, contemporary style, diction, and signature, which are accomplished and memorable in their own right:

> When they see me rise, a nebula of coronas, sun-
> burst spires strewn among their bluegrass lawns,
> they will come for me. When my roots fan a maze
> around their chrysanthemums, interlace a cage
> around their petunias, grab the life I'm so often denied,
> they will come for me…

The clever "Speaks" poems ache with startling extended metaphors and are rich in imagery and musicality. Their portrayals of the Black American and other experiences invite all of us to touch, to learn, to respect, to respond.

In summary, there is so much to admire and enjoy in *The Dandelion Speaks of Survival*. It easily earns a revered space on our bookshelves. We can all look forward to much more poetic genius from Quintin Collins, whose second manuscript has already won a major award and is forthcoming in 2022.

LISA ALLEN

Review: *Hue & Cry* by Diane K. Martin
MadHat Press 2020

When I read a poetry collection, particularly a collection from a poet whose work I don't yet know, I do what I heard Terrance Hayes say he does: I read the title poem first.

In Diane K. Martin's collection *Hue & Cry,* that poem comes in section three, page 45. It's a five chapter/section/stanza poem written in a pattern adapted from "Shine" by Sylvia Curbelo. It is, to me, an offering of five variations of one poem—five voices, maybe, or five perspectives. Five histories or five tellings, maybe.

In each chapter/section/stanza of this title poem, the voice is collective and the poem is delivered in direct address, the last line of each chapter/section/stanza speaking to an unnamed "you:"

> We hated breaking our promises.
> We couldn't enter or exit. (from variation 1)

> We hated the sound of our own names.
> We couldn't imagine an ending. (from variation 2)

> We hated being mistaken for tourists in our own country.
> We couldn't go backward or forward. (from variation 3)

> We hated to admit our pleasure.
> We couldn't have stilled its birth. (from variation 4)

> We hated to think of the big picture.
> We couldn't do anything by crawl on our bellies. (from variation 5)

The phrase "hue and cry" means a loud public clamor or outcry. In common law, it's a process in which bystanders—by definition, people who have no part in a story other than to watch/see/hear/feel it—are asked to help apprehend a criminal in the act of committing a crime. A citizen's arrest, so to speak.

That a good number of the poems in Martin's collection are persona poems written in the imagined voices of the women in Pablo Picasso's life might suggest that it's their voices that are clamoring for assistance. That the majority of these women—and Picasso—have died means there can be no holding to account. I will refrain here from veering into historical fact (Martin says, "My Picasso women poems, while true in spirit, are not intended as historical or wholly biographical documents." Page 93): that Picasso used women and tossed them aside when they ceased being/doing whatever it was he required of them. His granddaughter, Marina Picasso, is often quoted as saying, "He submitted them to his animal sexuality, tamed them, bewitched them, ingested them, and crushed them onto his canvas. After he had spent many nights extracting their essence, once they were bled dry, he would dispose of them."

That most certainly justifies hue and cry.

However, this poetry collection isn't strictly about the women in Picasso's life. As Martin writes in the acknowledgement section, what began as a weariness of writing about herself turned to reading about Picasso, which turned to fascination with Picasso and the women in his life. That grew into poems written in these women's voices, which in turn became a way to write about creativity and art—and the pursuit of both.

So the hue and cry of this collection, then, is perhaps less a call to judgment than it is a witnessing. In former English law, the call had to be raised not just to see a criminal brought to justice, but to assure the witness(es) wouldn't be held liable for damages suffered by the victim(s). And isn't that what we seek when we pick up a book, no matter its genre: to witness another life, another experience, another reality—to validate it, to document it, to learn from it as we keep moving, lest we contribute to the damage already done?

Back to that habit of reading the title poem of a collection first: when I do this, it sets an expectation of what I can expect to read as I return to the opening poem and begin. Here, my expectations were these: there will be a chorus of voices in this collection, not a solitary note;   there will be danger and uncertainty ("We craved safety and order./Elsewhere people had mothers, their mothers had children." from variation 2); there will be questions ("Haven't you ever wanted to be innocent? (from variation 1), "Haven't you ever wanted to walk on water?" (from variation 5).

It didn't take long before I saw, too, that there would be conversation. Consider the first three lines of the poem "Life Drawing," on page 77:

> Some are born to it,
> but you must acquire
>
> that innocence. You want
>
> *Haven't you ever wanted to be innocent?*
> *You must acquire that innocence you want.*

Martin's poems in this collection speak to each other, but they also speak to us—as in, I can read the "you" in the title poem as any of the women in the poems in the collection, or as myself. In most cases, each option opens the poems up in different ways, which are my favorite kind of poems to read. And there's another perk: I don't have to know everything about Picasso or the women in his life to feel these poems. Sure, I know *of* Picasso and his life—broad strokes, not the way Martin does, but enough to know he was prolific and inventive as a creative but brutal and abusive as a man. But the poems in *Hue & Cry* don't exclude me from the emotions Martin reveals, even when written in the persona of women I'll never know—because I know of shame, of spite, of jealousy, of devotion.

And it's here that this collection is at its best, in my opinion—in the voices of women not solely in Picasso's orbit. Like the voice of Eve in "Life Drawing," the Bag Lady in "Bag Lady's Song," (page 70) and, especially, the woman in "Piece of Work" (page 23):

> The night is almost too quiet.
> His snore is the exhaust of a semi
> roaring down the two-lane. The dog
>
> at her water bowl is a summer lake
> lapping the silt beach. And the woman
> —big glasses, denim jeans, hair

> pulled back with a scarf—holds
>
> a yellow pencil in her teeth.
>
> The woman is the poem.

The point isn't to cast the male as the villain. The point is to acknowledge, I think, that in homes famous and unknown, throughout time, in every unique family/romantic/working dynamic, women have been considered/written about as muses/lovers/spouses/others—especially, but not exclusively, when they share space with famous men—rather than creatives in their own right. Martin acknowledges this, particularly in the Picasso women persona poems, each of which is different, just as each woman was different.

Consider the first stanza of "Françoise Gilot: *La femme-fleur,* 1946:" (page 65)

> He laughed when we met, said I was too pretty
>
> to be a painter. Later, he conceded I had a gift,
>
> urged me to keep working, and invited me to show
>
> him my work from time to time. That's how

Françoise Gilot, as of this writing, is 99 years old. She is an artist and still paints every day—and has done so to critical acclaim (though she says that she doesn't care if anyone else likes her work; she paints for herself[1]). Yet, the first thing that shows up after an online search of her name is a Wiki panel that says: "Marie Françoise Gilot is a French painter, best known for her long, stormy relationship with Pablo Picasso, with whom she had two children."

Best known for her relationship with Picasso, for being the mother of two of his children.

He laughed when we met, said I was too pretty to be a painter.

Haven't you ever wanted to escape the body's prison? ("Hue & Cry," variation 4)

Haven't you ever wanted to elude destiny? ("Hue & Cry," variation 3)

---

[1] https://www.curbed.com/2020/10/inside-artist-francoise-gilots-apartment-and-art-studio.html

J.D. SCRIMGEOUR

Review: *All Morning the Crows* by Meg Kearney
The Word Works Press (2021)

> It was a crow first taught me
> how to pry a thing open—snatch
> a stick to leverage a headstone or widen
> the hole in a rotten pine's trunk
> to get at the story inside.
>   from "Crow" in Meg Kearney's *All Morning the Crows*

Meg Kearney's *All Morning the Crows*, the winner of the Word Works 2020 Washington Prize, consists of 51 poems in four sections, each poem titled with a bird's name and using facts, stories or observations about the species to reflect upon the human world. In the poems, Kearney confronts secrets in her own life and family history. Birds, like the crow above, are her tools that enable her to pry open difficult facts and weave her discoveries into the nest of narrative, something that can hold and sustain a self.

Kearney's previous collections, *An Unkindness of Ravens, Home By Now,* and *The Ice Storm,* gave glimpses of the life that gets sketched in *All Morning the Crows*. Her birth mother, a nun who left her convent, gave Kearney up for adoption, and she was raised in the small town of LaGrange, New York. While she grew up in a loving family, her mother's alcoholism made her absent at times, and Kearney struggled with substance abuse and unhealthy relationships, connected to—one senses—our culture's warped gender dynamics.

In her introduction to the collection, Kearney acknowledges she's not an official "birder," but that she's been "a lifelong lover of birds." Kearney's also a lover of narrative. She considers herself a narrative poet, and so it's not surprising that she found inspiration for her book from Diana Wells' *100 Birds and How They Got Their Names.* Like Wells' work, Kearney's poems write the story behind a name, such as the story of her birth mother, whom she never met, but only learned about as an adult, years after the mother had died of cancer.

> If you leave us, the nuns in Bristol
> told my first mother,
> you will die a terrible death.
> But she stole a dress blue

    as a baby crow's eye
    plus five hundred nickels.
              "Crow"

The book has two kinds of absent mothers, Kearney's "first mother," whom she never met, and the mother who raised her, who occasionally disappeared into the bottle. Both mothers haunt the book, although over the four sections, the narrative thread shifts its focus to the life of the daughter and her troubles. Interestingly, absence doesn't equate with neglect. The narrator admires the pluck of the "first mother" who escapes, and appreciates the flawed mother who raised her. In the poem, "Bluebird," in the book's final section, both mothers reappear in the speaker's dreams, the first is "happy" that the speaker has found the mother's other children, the second "took my hand and there it was//a gleaming sapphire, warm/to the touch and throbbing with what felt/like desire."

Kearney's poems are not all autobiographical, but even those that focus on other lives, such as the pantoum, "Penguins," reflect major themes in the autobiographical story: abandonment, violence, haunting. The poem tells of how sailors slaughter "a cluster of fathers and their chicks" who are "waiting for the mother penguins' return." At the poem's end, the sailors' dreams are haunted by the fact that "penguins look like little children."

The book's epigraph is two definitions of the word "bird" from the O.E.D.. One is "the general name for the young of a feathered tribe," and the other is "A maiden, a girl...In modern (revived use) a girl, woman (often used familiarly, disparagingly) (slang)."And a major strand of the book is how birds are treated, how they learn to survive (or, sometimes, don't) in this world.

Here's the protagonist describing an attic apartment she had as a young woman:

                                                        ...swifts
streamed by her skylight like a ribbon, twisted, then lifted up
and east toward town. By dusk they were funneling above

the chimneys, six crumbling roosts the second floor boys planned
to raid should they discover a recipe for swift soup, the boys
students at the Culinary Institute, drawn to menus of the unusual
and bizzare. "Flying cigars," they nicknamed those birds, blunt

heads and squared off tails color of dried tobacco. When she lit
a spliff, cranked ZZ Top, the boys pounded on her trapdoor to come
up.
                "Swifts"

So much gets accomplished here—the beauty of the swifts in flight, the sinister boys and their constant threat, and the speaker's own youthful life of spliffs and ZZ Top. We feel, richly, deeply, the jittery isolation of the protagonist.

Things don't get better. The misery of bad relationships is compounded by addiction: "Bird shit will strip paint off your truck/ as sure as your ex cleaned you out/ of near everything you owned" ("Barn Swallows"). Kearney tempers this bleakness with a wry voice that establishes a useful distance from the poem's subjects. Describing another ex, she writes "When he promised her music, he'd meant/ the store-bought kind, the brand that comes in a can" ("Ostrich").

In the book's last section, the poems, and the protagonist, find a certain peace. There's a provisional quality to this peace, perhaps because it is cobbled together from several sources: a good partner, a good dog, the serenity of a home In the White Mountains, and faith. Yet that tenuousness makes the triumphs all the more moving. In "Fundevogel," a poem in Kearney's previous book, *Home By Now*, the restless narrator is spoken to by her "dead father" and gives an agonized reply:

> Margaret, he says, it's time to sleep. But
> Father, what to do about this meddlesome
> crow, pecking at my window?

In this book, Kearney has found an answer to that "meddlesome crow." She has turned it into art and the salvation it can offer.

ERIC E. HYETT

Review: *Unholy Heart* by Grace Bauer
Nebraska Press, 2021

Reading *Unholy Heart*, the 169-page compendium of new and selected poems by Grace Bauer (poems spanning an arc of nearly 30 years) is a unique opportunity to get to know Ms. Bauer, and to witness the development of her funny, thoughtful, highly-original poetic voice. Due to the decades that elapse, and the breadth of subjects covered, the book gives the reader the sense of Bauer's own story, and the unique poetic voice that has grown alongside her. "Unholy Heart" begins with selected poems from an early Bauer book, "The Women At The Well," first published in 1996. You'll notice right away that Bauer's poem titles (throughout "Unholy Heart" and also in this section), are everything a poem title should be: narrative, funny, surprising. They draw the reader in. In "Noah's Wife Addresses The Department of the Interior," I was hooked by the feminist humor with which she approaches bible stories:

> Giraffes are a pain
> in the neck to feed.
> Try it once, you'll see.

The same wry wit appears in "Martha to Mary: The Quotidian Demands of the Flesh" which begins:

> I remember well when Jesus
> said we do not live
> by bread alone, but I *don't*
> think he was telling us
> we need not ever cook.

These approachable persona poems, all spoken in the voices of women of the bible, are funny, serious, and in this context, they set up the basic questions Bauer returns to throughout *Unholy Heart*. Questions about faith, and art, and how we evolve in response to lived experience. Questions about the places we take root in, that take root in us.

The selections from *Retreats and Recognitions* (Lost Horse Press, 2007) showcase Bauer's love of poetic forms, including a willingness to break form and use it *only* to serve the poem's interests (a sign of true mastery). I loved the inventive 17-line sonnet, "Note from the Imaginary Daughter." There's a perfect sestina called "A Little Like Dorothy" which sets up the speaker's move to Nebraska (a little like Kansas?). There is more persona, and then a breakthrough poem, "Retreat" which stands out for being so exquisitely personal.

Everything comes together in a ghazal called "Plot Lines" where Bauer's use of "tale/tail/cocktail" as her repeat means the poem is always moving and changing. In order to get her own name into the penultimate line as required by the form, Grace Bauer ends with this couplet:

> I want my poems to be graceful, do I fail?
> *Her reach exceeds her grasp.* Oh, that old tale.

By this point, I was pretty much in love with Bauer's warmth and lighthearted creativity, as well as responding to the craftwork she obviously put in. I could compare her to a number of well-known female poets, but she's got her own, jazzy thing going on, and it works for her. In a poem called "Latter Day Saints" Bauer's speaker hilariously frightens off some Mormon missionaries. And in "On Finding a Footnote to *Truckin'*" she defends her generation:

> I am, after all, of that generation
> that *trucked* through the sixties. One of those
> *boomers* who elevated *freak* into a compliment
> and turned *party* into a verb...

In the poems selected from *Beholding Eye* (CustomWords, 2006) ekphrasis and persona are Bauer's chosen devices. When she deploys them simultaneously, the effect is gorgeous: an intimate telling from a carefully-calibrated distance. Bauer inhabits Frida Kahlo ("Frida Digresses on Red"), Georgia O'Keeffe ("Georgia, at Ninety, Learns To Make a Vessel"). Also in this section, a glaringly-perfect villanelle called "For Her Villain" (what a title!).

Bauer becomes her contemporary self in the selections from *Nowhere All At Once* (Stephen F. Austin State University Press, 2014). "Bless us, Oh Lord, //and this our Jell-O" is the opening to "Great Plains Prayer." It becomes clear (and stays clear throughout the rest of "Unholy Heart") that Nebraska is now Bauer's long-term home, and she begins to put down roots there. The stanzas are more rectangular in shape, "repeating *square, square, square,*" she writes, mirroring the Nebraska geography. "Against Lawn" is one of the most lyrically-beautiful poems in this section.

There is another fabulous ghazal, "Gray Ghazal" with another great use of the poet's name which I won't spoil here. And I loved "Unrepentant Prayer," which opens:

> Bless me, father, for I have sinned,
> my last confession was ten poems ago...

The selections from *MEAN/TIME* (University of New Mexico Press, 2017) feature a jazzy wordplay paired with a mysterious, unnamed second-person speaker. "You" is the predominant pronoun in this section; there's the occasional "we" or "our" but absolutely never an "I." The use of second-person reads as a dissociative tool used to distance the speaker from her own experiences. The effect is lovely, as in a poem called "The Wandering Dream"

> And leaving is what you are all about.
> Headed somewhere toward or away
> from wherever it is you are now.

In the section called "New Poems" that concludes *Unholy Heart*, Ms. Bauer loses her father, and the reader starts to read the "we" in the poems as her family. Where the *MEAN/TIME* poems are deliberately distanced so as to create beauty, the New Poems are intimate and personal. In "Provisions for the Journey," Ms. Bauer is present when her father receives his last rites. It is not a metaphor for anything, just a poem whose power is grounded in witnessing a hard truth.

The book concludes with thoughtful notes, and the word "generous" that appears twice on the back cover. I could not agree more: *Unholy Heart* has a lot to give.

JENNIFER MARTELLI

Review: *Loosen* by Kyle Potvin
Hobblebush Books, 2021

In her poem, "Like a Wasp In the Wall," Kyle Potvin writes

> Go small.
>
> Shed the fur of your home
> and the lawn of gnawed bones.
>
> Don't whimper as your fingers loosen
> on Lessing and Murdoch and Kenyon.

The poems in Potvin's collection, *Loosen*, insist that we look closely and within at the smallest objects: a wasp, a snarl in a necklace chain, a crack in a crystal glass, a cancer cell. The poet tightens the lens, and we gaze deeper at the inner stitching, at a legacy of motherhood and poetic craft. Using this precision to hone her poetic needles, Potvin's focus is on the sharp truth and the most accurate rhyme.

The poems in *Loosen* begin with tiny web-like cracks, and grow; their expanse threatens to swallow the reader as well as the speaker.

> You are light, unencumbered
> as the crystal glass you now fill.
>
> Your mother and grandmother drank from it too,
> with roses, buds and blooms, acid-etched.

Potvin's use of form and rhyme underscores how cruelly exact and obsessive cancer is. In "Do You Know Pain," she writes

> The prick of the needle
> Poison-plumped veins
> White sores in the mouth
> Cold fog in the brain.

As I read this book, I found myself—an inveterate marker of books—writing in tiny letters, with a micro-nib pen, then shifting to a larger scrawl, mimicking the tempo, or the tidal nature, of these poems. Much like cancer, the focus starts microscopically, then grows under the surface. Potvin includes perfect Elizabethan sonnets throughout *Loosen*, adhering to the strict rhyme scheme of the sonnet. By using this strict form, Potvin pays homage to a deep poetic past, grown weighty with the years. In her sonnet, "The New Normal" Potvin begins with

> To grow a Texas cactus from the start,
> You scatter tiny seeds on dirty and sand
> (Your nail works well to nudge the stuck ones apart).

The roots of this poem are revealed in the final ending couplet, "The victory is all my own: Mom's hair?/The news is we grew a Prickly Pear." In "The Hard Work of Dying," the sonnet form allows for this balance of precision, with the smallest bits of food, and the depth of roots:

> Ten days since Emma took a sip of tea
> or ate a slice of grape. She sleeps while the rain
> whispers a soothing chatter. The oak tree
> clears its throat, weeping acorns in the drain.
> Yellow snapdragons brighten up the room
> A day from now they'll see a second bloom.

Food—eating and growing it—is a constant image in *Loosen*. The act of swallowing (painful or nauseating during cancer treatments) allows for another inside view. Potvin presents food as a way to show depth and growth of cancer; but sometimes health and regeneration as well. In "Ramps," a paean to the wild leek, she writes

> Your season is brief
> yet you are complicated,
> three parts in one:
> pungent bulb that hides
> beneath the surface, magenta stem,
> broad tender leaf that disappears by summer.

As I read the poem, I returned over and over to the line ". . . bulb that hides/beneath the surface," and thought of a cruel disease and how it sneaks into a life as a "dirty" cell, something small, yet deep and "complicated." Potvin transforms the trauma of cancer into something exotic in "Chayote Fruit," when the speaker feels this fruit "with a bumpy skin" and draws "my hand/to my chest."

The violence of surgery follows when

>at the next stall
>a mall with a machete
>cleaves a coconut,
>removes a useless piece . . . .

Potvin uses images of jewelry—necklaces, beads, earrings—to embody the sense of a life, of a connectedness, and of consequence. The last and title poem, "Loosen," which is a directional poem about unloosening knots or snarls in a neckless is pulled throughout the book, not only from the cover to the last page, but also by using individual stanzas to introduce each of the book's five sections. Again, Potvin uses this image as a way to express the weight and length of a life, the nature of these snarls, and how this chain links to history and progeny. The poem, which opens the first section, tells us

>For years I suffer snarls
>in my expensive necklace.
>I wear these knots daily.

The knots are "too tight," representing things "you can't forget." These knots require precision, wounds, sharp tools:

>For thirty years, the woman
>carries sutures inside her. One day,
>she realizes they dissolved long ago.

This poem is an entrance into a body, which is more than its disease diagnosis: it is a DNA chain; it is genetic, carrying not just cancer, but a life. Potvin relies on these images of chains and beads to give a sense of length or really, perspective. The speaker recognizes her own place in the genetic chain, as a granddaughter, daughter, and mother. Like a chain, every link is essential; there's no room for a broken piece. Potvin's sharp couplet poem, "The Next Time Called," relies on the Rosary and its obsessive repetitive beads to illustrate genetics:

>In Baptism.
>Eucharist. Rosary.
>
>Makes a choice.
>Has no choice.

> Has a daughter
> who could be BRCA 1, BRCA 2.

Despite the fear inherent in a cancer diagnoses, Potvin relies on these tiniest adornments that portend health and a continuation of a genetic chain. In her poem, "Advice for My Future Granddaughter When I Give Her Diamond Earrings for Her 25th Birthday," Potvin "tangles" a story of her youth with a projection for a later generation:

> Later that night—morning really—
> be careful removing your tank top
> so you do not dislodge one of those diamond earrings.
>
> Although with any luck you will find it on the floor in the morning,
> winking when the sun catches it.

Kyle Potvin illuminates these most precious and smallest of gems. *Loosen* goes beyond the boundaries of cancer; this is a book about breath and precision and lifetimes. "I choose needles, on point/anchoring, another teasing/apart the tightness." Kyle Potvin uses her poetry as needles. As I read *Loosen*, I could feel myself tightening and loosening within each poem; constricting, then growing larger to take in more than just the words on the page. *Loosen* will stay with me for a long time, as if the poet took a sharp knife to "scratch a K into the wood and leave."

KALI LIGHTFOOT

Review: *The Taste of the Earth* by Hedy Habra
Press 53

Hedy Habra's third collection of poetry, *The Taste of the Earth* was the winner of the 2020 Silver Nautilus Book Award in Poetry, also a Grand Prix 2020 Shortlist Honoree in all genres for the Eric Hoffer Award, and Finalist for the 2019 Best Book Award in Poetry.

The first lines of "Topography," the initial poem in the book, describe the poet contemplating her own reflection in a mirror:

> Sometimes I think my face is a map,
> each line a faint record of hidden scars,
> of what I've seen or felt…

and the poem ends with this sentence:

> …I often see
> that other face beneath the one looking
> at me in the mirror, swelling with recollections,
> unraveling all of my senses.

Indeed, the topography found in the book itself is a combination of internal and external mapping, as Habra sifts through her memories of places lived in and left, some long ago, some torn by war and upheaval.

Hedy Habra identifies herself as "of Lebanese origin…born and raised in Heliopolis, Egypt and has lived in both countries." (hedyhabra.com) Her first language was French, and she is now fluent in five languages plus having studied both Greek and Latin. In Beirut she graduated with a B.S. in Pharmacy, but left Lebanon at the start of the civil war, spent time in Athens Greece, six years in Brussels, Belgium, and then settled in Kalamazoo, Michigan where she earned an M.A. and M.F.A in English and an M.A. and Ph.D. in Spanish Literature from Western Michigan University, where she now teaches. This might seem like the biography of a linguist in love with words, but that is only a part of Habra's story. She also has a passion for, and broad knowledge of painting. The cover of *The Taste of the Earth* is Habra's own painting "The Sons of Horus," and she is currently studying Mandarin Chinese and Chinese Ink Brush Painting.

The Taste of the Earth is organized in five sections. The first is a kind of introduction to themes and concerns of the collection, and also a tasting menu of various poetic forms Habra uses in the later sections: stanzaed columns, tercets, couplets, haibun, and interesting placements of lines on a page—the painterly linguist's eye confronting white space.

Section II takes the reader to the oldest inhabited city in the world, Jbeil, Byblos, where Habra in her introduction to "Meditations Over Phoenician Letters," points out their nature as "visual messages that sailed from shore to shore undergoing an alchemical transformation, still echoing the same sounds in other tongues." Each drawing of a letter is followed by a brief lyrical response.

Section IV returns to meditations, this time "Meditations Over the Eye of Horus," the "*Wadjet*, the most powerful of protective amulets" in ancient Egypt. Each poem in the section is a haibun, a Japanese form that combines a short prose paragraph with a classic haiku, and the form is often used to record a journey. Habra is a published author of prose, both fiction and essay—as well as a poet—and the haibun form makes excellent use of her talents. Each haibun responds to a part of the shattered eye of Egyptian god Horus and one of the senses: smell, sight, thought, hearing, taste, touch. From the 4th part of *Sam* (hearing):

…Emanations of jasmine and honeysuckle mixed with fragments of dialogues. Moonlight filtered through shutters would turn the ceiling into a live screen on which we'd stage our own script.

broken words shiver.
a double flame undulates
in chiaroscuro.

Within this consideration of an ancient symbol, using another country's ancient form, Habra creates poems that recall moments of joy and sorrow, family memories, personal experience, and world history. Each sense—and part of Horus' eye—ends with a list poem:

the sight of Poinciana's lush flames, their yellow
    stamen in flight
the sight of the Nile glittering in the felucca's wake
    under the moonlight
the sight of the woman's blue bra uncovered
    as she was beaten in Tahrir Square
the sight of …

For all of the rich sensory engagement, affecting detail, and simple beauty of Section IV, the heart of this collection might reside in Section III, within the poem "Weaving and Unweaving" which sits among others that reflect on the poet's memories of civil war and displacement from Lebanon. The poem starts by echoing the unraveling in "Topography":

> I used to marvel at my mother's readiness
> to unravel a sweater
> or unstitch
>
> her needlepoint
> at the slightest error…

then asks "But why look at unweaving as erasure…" and after exploring aspects of weaving and unweaving, Habra ends the poem with:

> …The image
>
> vanishes, not the roads that led to it,
> like a text whose lines haunt you…
>
> A constant wavering between
> remembering and forgetting,
> telling and retelling.

The Taste of the Earth is far more than "taste" in the work of a woman whose restless intellect and ability to express sensory details creates so many poems that soar and yet are grounded in her experience. In an interview on *The Next Big Thing* blog hop, posted at her website, hedyhabra.com, Habra speaks of her first books *Tea in Heliopolis* (poetry), and *Flying Carpets* (short stories) as "an attempt to recover people, places, affects pertaining to an almost mythical past that is at the same time lost yet alive…"—a past that remains alive in this fine collection of poems. Whether or not you have ever tasted *zaatar*, Turkish coffee, Belgian waffles, or good Midwestern tuna noodle casserole, your own senses and memories will come alive as you read this book—an experience not to be missed.

M. P. CARVER

Review: Pelted by Flowers by Kali Lightfoot
CavanKerry Press, 2021

> "The apples will not care
> that I didn't walk this morning
> or never learned a second language
> or read Proust
> or was not a better supervisor."
>   —From "Star Stuff" pg. 81

Pelted by Flowers, the debut collection by poet Kali Lightfoot, is a wide-reaching portrait of a life in the world, touching on personal memory and identity without shying away from nature, society, or even the philosophical. The opening poem, "Cousin Margaret's Friend, 1955" re-examines childhood memories of a lesbian relationship that wasn't spoken about openly, with all the satisfying undertones that a child might recognize but not understand:

> Later my dad and the friend went out back,
> laughing together, ripping the husks
> from coconuts on a sharpened metal stake,
> tall and lethal…".

After being pulled into these descriptions, I was struck when the adult perspective came in towards the end,

> Half my life went by before I understood.
> Now I too have loved a woman and lost
> her to death. But not to silence—".

Lightfoot continues to use this contrast between changing perspectives to great effect throughout the book, which is filled with moments well described, in poems about early childhood, developing sexuality and lesbian identity, and career changes, to name just a few. Lightfoot is not afraid to let a bit of darkness show, "A gut twisting sense of wrongness warred with my pleasure / of touching her body. I stayed away from her for all the next day, / rode my bike to the library, and for the first time felt afraid of myself."

Even in a poem about the approaching death of a former love, the poems let a little reality and playfulness into the reflections, "The day I moved out, we said / good-bye, and hugged—sadly / civilized women making the best." Whether it's from personal sensibility or her perspective as an older writer, Lightfoot deftly navigates moments another poet might have leaned into as trauma and has brought forth a collection both deep and gratifying. This approach also allows her to work in poems about lighter topics, lesbian romance novels, nature-channel like observations of Salem in tourist season, and one of my personal favorites about troublesome porcupines that ends with the speaker "Crazed primate, wilderness guard, protector of wildlife," hurling creek stones alone and naked in the dark woods of Oregon. Another striking poem is "Three Seals", a triptych from which the book takes its title. The poem begins with the speaker on the steps of City Hall in Portland, ME, seeing the first legally recognized gay marriage in the U.S., one with the crowd watching the couple "pelted by flowers" and cheering, "our voices husky with cold." In the next section, the speaker is in a solo canoe in Boothbay Harbor in the "quiet of the purple dawn," but even here the speaker finds connection, this time with a nearby harbor seal, "We breathe together awhile."

In the final section, the speaker in Salem, MA approaches "Our post office" to mail "another donation I can't afford—", and even in this act finds connection, "unheard, unseen; what to do but lick the envelope, / seal my cheek inside, stop at the bronze slot / and tip the flap, feel a puff of air as my hopes / land with all the others there in the dark."

The triptych is not long yet it is expansive, and, like the collection, takes the reader with deceptive ease through time, space, themes, even the personal and the external of the poet's "much worried, much loved life".

NEIL LEADBEATER

Review: *Ash* by Gloria Mindock
Glass Lyre Press, 2021

As I write this review, wildfires are raging across southern Europe and certain sections of the North American continent. Fire is a destructive force that is hard to tame, even spreading through this latest collection of poetry from poet, editor and publisher, Gloria Mindock, who was Poet Laureate in Somerville, MA during the period 2017-2018.

The collection comprises sixty poems divided into four sections. The alliterative headings of the first three of these sections (Burnt, Baked, Buried) are as stark as the titles of her poems, many of which simply consist of a single word. They give us a hint of Mindock's direct, no-nonsense style. The final section, headed 'Opposition' pitches one person against another in relationships that are complicated and riddled with conflict. Here again, the text is sparse.

What are we to make of the title? Ash is the dust or remains of anything that has been burnt. It is all about disintegration, a word that appears several times throughout this collection. Alongside the words 'fire' and 'flame', the word 'heart' appears more prominently than any other: it is used at least thirty times. It underlines the fact that this is a book dealing with human relationships and that the fire burning through its pages is more metaphorical than literal. The heart, after all, is the seat of the emotions, the part of the body that houses our innermost thoughts and affections.

With the exception of the first poem and the whole of Section IV where individuals are referred to anonymously by a single alphabetical letter, Mindock generally makes use of the first person singular but it should be pointed out that these poems do not in any way relate to her own personal life, they are a collection of stories about other people and their relationships as told to her.

Where do you begin when a past relationship is nothing more than a burnt-out shell? In 'Missile' Mindock provides the chilling answer: 'there is a smoldering that never goes out'. Although the focus of the collection is mainly about relationships between two people, Mindock widens the scope of her subject matter which is largely concerned with the brutal, darker side of human nature, to ask in general terms : 'Why is there such violence? / Hate?' The word 'hate' is given a line all to itself as if to emphasise the extent of its presence in the world and the enormity of its consequences.

If all this sounds overpowering, there is in evidence a seam of dark humour that runs through many of these poems. It is present in the opening sequence of prose poems titled 'Plastic' and it is particularly evident in poems such as 'Baked', 'Escape' and 'Ticket' where the sarcasm is searing:

> Come get your ticket to expire.
> Your lover wants you.
> Take this drug, he says, it is good for you.
> It only has 10 side effects –
> if you're lucky, you will never forget me.
> It will cripple you or kill you with yearning.
> If you feel numbness or start to die,
> go to the nearest ER.
> Whoops, too late.
> Guess you shouldn't have taken the pills.

Not everything in this collection is dark. Remember those wildfires that raged through the bush in Australia? Not everything died. Green shoots very quickly began to appear out of the scorched earth. Any farmer will tell you that stubble is burnt for a reason. In mythology, the phoenix rose out of the ashes. So too, here, Mindock provides us with hope. In 'Air' she writes, 'Not everyone believes in destruction. / All the heart wants is to beat' and in 'Crawling Stones' the victim of an unhappy liaison, after she had cast her burdens into the river, 'soared / like a bird, flying across the water, singing.'

In the final section, titled 'Opposition' each of the seven titles is represented by a letter of the alphabet, followed by a forward slash which is then followed by another letter of the alphabet, e.g. A/K; J/M; etc. The letters refer to individuals and the use of the forward slash is the membrane between them that is about to burst, the lines of demarcation that cannot be crossed under any circumstances. Each poem, which consists of two short stanzas, is presented with an air of detachment, directly opposing what has gone before. They are all framed in the past tense, and are cast as if being reviewed by a third party. In each of them, Mindock exposes a catalogue of faults and human failings.

Mindock's poems are models of concision. She chooses her words carefully. Part of the reason why these poems are so powerful is because they convey a lot of emotion in a confined space. She writes with conviction, revealing the depth of her understanding as she exposes our vulnerability with surgical precision.

It is often hard to write convincingly about something which conveys both comedy and tragedy at one and the same time. If it is not done well, the one tends to diminish the other with equal force. One of the many strengths of this collection is that Mindock manages to find the right balance between the two and walks the tightrope without falling off. Fully recommended.

CAROL HOBBS

Review: *The Animal at Your Side* by Megan Alpert
Airlie Press, 2020

Megan Alpert creates in *The Animal at Your Side* a wondrous map with an organizing legend topographical in its first three sections – "Trails," "Shores," "Interiors" – then suggesting less structured movements – "Out Further" and "Ways in the Dark." Alpert invites the reader along on this trek through transformations and connections among humans and animals of the natural world as she simultaneously pulls on supernatural threads with the dead returning to guide and advise the living. Much of her subject matter is delivered by a poet-migrant moving away from and back to family and historic places, and then observing the migration of populations uprooted by war and industrialization.

In "Dawn," the initial poem of the collection, Alpert meets her beloved dead, a sister and grandmother, posing the central question of the bereaved: "Will I wake anywhere/besides this house, /or love anyone ever/beyond my sister/with her skinned knees?" This sister "smelling of dirt she was buried in" returns again and again, sometimes speaking directly to the poet and sometimes recalled in narratives as in "Seven Years" when the poet rejects the slippage of time since the sister's death, "the yellow dot of her/folded into a map." This poem inserts a childhood memory of falling backwards into snow to watch their breath "written/ on the air...." The sister comes again in "A Vacancy" as a story struggling to be told true "through the eyes/of a sister that never was," and rises mythic in "One Must Go," battling whatever there is out there while the poet stays home with the dog, that animal at her side who smells of both home and the sister's body bloodied from battle. The transformations of human to myth to animal meet in the poet's hand, "my animal hand alive in the dog's fur."

Transformation settles on the image of a tree becoming a deer as invoked in the poem "Ayil," in Hebrew meaning both oak tree and stag, which also offers the title line. The tree aflame reveals the "antlers at the center." Breaking definitional boundaries is a through line of this book. "In Wolf Country" finds the tree and deer skull "licked clean by dogs" as a wolf is kept from surfacing in the bearded and shaved cheek of a lover. The poet caresses her lover's transitioned self, tracing "sickle scars where [their] breasts were." But the lover wants to "transition without symbols" as they file down the points of their teeth. There is violence underlying the stories of women who "left the path" as in "A Guide" where fairytale breadcrumbs get eaten and the woman is changed from a speaker to "the body" reported on the evening news. This figure transforms into "What rises.../half-animal, look[ing] out the sides of its eyes" as it searches the "the hollowed-out rut in the leaves." All that remains is that negative space where the body existed, another iteration of transition from human to animal/spirit to empty place in the landscape.

Alpert's journeys intricately trace geography with the most arresting placement in the Ecuadorian rainforest. "Village at the End of the Oil Road" follows the poet as she recognizes herself in a bird fed katydids by the caretaker at the oil camp. She ponders the transitioned word for "outsider" from "cannibal" to "the one we have to feed so they do not starve." She is cared for by women who feed her and teach her how to wash her clothes in "the only clean river." The outsiders fence off the jungle, redraw the known landscapes. "Reporting from Oil Block 16" finds the poet and a journalist in the back of a pickup which scares away animals along the oil road back to camp. The conversation flits between Spanish and English and forms a quick intimacy: "Mi corazón... (in Spanish you can say this to a stranger)." Human relationships become corrupted, the journalist's marriage, and corruption obliterates understanding of the traditional landscape, "pipelines hidden/behind trees whose names and uses we did not know." This corruption brings pain with the "heavy weight of the tape recorder" on the poet's back. Alpert implores us to understand the position of outsider, specifically her empathy for the plight of the native peoples, who are dispossessed of their land and bodies by oil companies and Christianity, and her true desire to be past tense and not present in the land itself. In "Going to Palmyra" she considers the violence of this market town where "men bought rifles/to kill the family hiding from the oil roads," and where "nine-foot spears" are displayed in a chapel, evidence of an earlier resistance to Christian missionaries. By the end of the poem the poet is truly humbled, hoping her essay will "do good" but knowing "once published will change nothing." Alpert is true to her poetry, stating a wish and a correction, "I will still want to be here always/That's a lie/I will always want to have been here." This is heartbreaking editing for the truth of the thing.

The Animal at Your Side is a rare and beautiful book. I could go on to touch each poem here, but the brevity of a review does not permit me. You would do well to read this collection which most deservedly received the 2020 Airlie Prize. Megan Alpert is at all times vulnerable and fearless, a dichotomy necessary to reveal the interconnectedness of human, animal, place, and time. When she writes of her grandparents' home in Belarus as "a place they lived for a while," we understand how universally, we are passing through landscapes, eras, bodies, soil. These poems ask readers to travel the transforming routes and recognize themselves in the entirety.

KIRSTEN MILES

Body as Blade, a review of *Divine Divine Divine* by Daniel Summerhill
Nomadic Press, 2021

If "Language is a human way of knowing," as posed by linguist Nicholas Evans, then Daniel B Summerhill's *Divine Divine Divine* calls upon syntax to bend, shake, and dance a cadence across a eurocentric cannon and claim Black language as a force of strength, resistance, and love. His introductory poem, "concerning fire" invokes the gospel in traditional couplets, justice only possible through a sulphur strike of divine intervention.

> hard to imagine any other way of shedding light
> on injustice but through brimstone.

Summerhill traces an unfolding of oral power born of love and survival in the title poem, laying a blessing on a mother's worst fear, following each line with a typographic lightning strike, affirming the divine for each needless, devastating loss.

> ain't no mama allowing their baby to swing
> from a tree without divine permission //

Familiar forms are shattered across the page. The tempo and pulse of each poem stretches the conversation between content and space. In "preface before discourse on location" gesture is both tension and release between breath and fist. Music and language are tightly bonded in the soul's determination not to be defined by conflictand violence in "concerning: survival:"

> a body forged
> In war will always hunger for a language
> unviolent enough to sing inthis blues
> Is called
> Survival

Summerhill summons the moment of a young boy's confrontation with rejection of his language of survival and identity in *How to salt a wound*

> you survived
> The inflammation of 9th grade
> Literature by biting your tongue
> And watching your language
> Drip on the floor

He traces the progression of the call and response between a language hostile to the people it addressed, who transformed and wrenched it back, brilliantly in "aunt georgia makes fried chitlins"

> how then have we been able
>
> to take bile
>
> and digest it? to salt
>
> the distaste
>
> of *nigger,*
>
> drop the e and r,
>
> adding an a
>
> and spitting out
>
> *brother*
>
> In *broken english* the body becomes change.
>
> what happens to the mouth
>
> as it sculpts
>
> a new language?
>
> as the tongue finds
>
> new ways of ex-
>
> pressing its distaste
>
> for subjugation.

Titles are used as an alternate narrative; they carry the reader like a lattice over the poems they serve. The juxtaposition of "baritone body" followed by "while the praise team sings how great," leads the transition beneath the titles, from broken lines and bodies strewn across two pages, to:

> he doesn't know how to listen
>   to the gospel without his eyes
>   singing songs his heart
>   wished it didn't know

In "deluge" the son is witness to his aunt, to the gut punch, the rage and strength of mothers making homes and staying afloat on the thinnest of air. That rage becomes a body, becomes a blade and prayer " when a people mourn" and Summerhill takes that body back to challenge the traditional couplet again in "today's prayer" which becomes an ars poetica call for a people.

> Today's prayer is for peer review –
> Today's prayer is to revise and submit
>
> Today's prayer doesn't include
> Submission. Today's prayer is broadcast
>
> Today's prayer is for a self-sharpening body.

Summerhill closes with "an urban dictionary." Words cover the page on their own terms - a staccato declaration that a Black boy is a new tongue, a body held by divine love, a body made blade sharp and

>   is enough   grace
> and circling back to his beginning,
>
>   is hot water   just before it boils over.

Circling back, Summerhill reminded us in "concerning: fire" we must know it is hard to imagine being on the wrong side "of all this smoke."

GLORIA MONAGHAN

Review: *Manimal Woe* by Fanny Howe
Arrowsmith, 2021

What better way to connect with the dead than a direct address? Fanny Howe's latest book, *Manimal Woe*, begins as such:

> "Dear Daddy,
> Don't worry. I know you're dead."

Manimal Woe is a conversation with the reader as well as a reflection on the 20th century. The nature of the book is collaborative with drawings from artists, Colleen McCallion and Taylor Davis, as well as archived letters, and the ghost of the father regularly showing up in conversation. It is creative nonfiction, historical text, prose, poetry and memoir all in one, that never ceases to restore its readers to the present. The social and political names may have changed over the course of Howe's life, (as she astutely points out) but the problems are still here. Our endless desire to be free of them does not change the reality of where we are today.

The book is as much a conversation with herself as it is with her father, who speaks through her. She inserts his letters throughout, which were written to her from her rebellious teenage years until his sudden death in 1967. A year after his death she would marry Carl Senna, who is of African-Mexican descent and is also a poet and writer. They would go on to have three children together and divorce. She writes that ideas bound the couple together; ideas and books.

The central theme of the collection is desire for freedom, freedom from history, racial prejudice, gender inequality, the body, and memory. But the book never seeks to be free from the spiritual recognition of God. Fanny Howe's a mystical writer primarily interested in spirit and matter: the mutual and necessary relationship of the diurnal and the divine.

This collection meditates on, and explores the roots of a city from where she was raised, fled and returned to, only to find the endless complexities of racial, economic and religious strife more prominent than ever before she left. There is a connection to place that is childlike and esoteric:

"It was always hard for me to leave home, not because of family but because of the trees, bushes, robins, cardinals, yellow leaves, chipmunks, rabbits, lilacs, and other wildlife. These were abundant in Mount Auburn Cemetery where I played and now walk."

The letters (both imaginary and real) are filled with measured fatherly advice on his end that is rational and elegant. Her adolescent response? Wild and unapologetic.

"At night I had my marvelous, wonderful, extravagant, anarchist friends to walk the streets with me and Woofer, and I always loved to dance. But the assassinating- bullets made a hole in the Book of Our Days. Oh woe!"

If *Manimal Woe* is a love story to the 20th century, it is also a rumination on loss, a central theme being the burden that we carry from the injustices and mistakes of the past. Her father, who worked as a secretary to Justice Oliver Wendell Holmes Jr, was also his biographer.

"Critical race theory is an outgrowth of critical legal studies, itself a development in the tradition of American legal realism, the sociologically inflected school of legal history and theory with roots in Oliver Wendell Holmes Jr. 's 1881 *The Common Law*."

Manimal Woe begins with a epitaph from an essay Howe wrote called "Keepers of the Image" about two Polish sister poets who survived a Nazi concentration camp. Howe translated their poetry in her book, *A Wall of Two*. *Manimal Woe* ends with an image of a photo, which her sister Helen made as a headstone at the back of the book. In this way the book makes a full circle from the 20th to the 21th century. Helen Howe's words on the headstone dismiss the narrative of linear time:

> Yes, tomorrow he died
> I will stop being a child
> I will be able to
> bear anything
> I would have to
> wouldn't I

In our postmodern, postwar, postcolonial, posthuman world, the unavoidable truth is that poetry is the lexicon of history when all other truths fail. In preserving a life story, which is also the story of history, Howe writes: "He who knows how to grant comfort becomes the guarantor of hope, the keeper of one's image of oneself.." Howe's mysticism is revealed in her assurance that "Objects are donations given by invisible entities to our daily lives."

At times this memoir moves into an imaginary conversation between an unnamed interviewer and the poet. When asked what she likes about Christianity, she replies: "A beauty- filled vision of reality where there is a quiet that creates a resting place between the one who sees and the one who is seen." The inspiration (wind) which becomes words, then whirls back as soon as words are uttered, but the 'mystery survives.'

Fanny Howe's life seems to contradict all expectations from a girl child born in 1940 and raised in a patrician home in Cambridge, to a father who taught law at Harvard and a mother from Dublin who acted in the Abby Players. In an imaginary, undated letter written in the future to her dead father, Howe writes:

> "(I always had a dog: Woofer, Hippo, Anubis, Chubby, Dumpling, Ruby, Blue, and Ramona.) (I learned everything from dogs.) "

She became a Catholic convert after living with Senna's mother, who was herself a Catholic, like Simeone Weil, a writer Fanny has also written about. "Either begin with the infant or the dirt. Each one carries its origins into its designated future. One produces wheat, one water." Even that biblical image is tied to justice and inequality.

Fanny Howe writes: "I am using writing to show portions of a history that we shared and that took place at the level of protest against power: weak, barely heard but untiring."

She confronts her own Brahmin family history and finds it is not two dimensional but layered, due to men like her father who were from a distinct social class but not in it and this is bewildering for him and for her, "He saluted during the National Anthem at Red Sox games." This kind of person has almost vanished from history. After serving in the war in Africa and Italy, he was labelled in the McCarthy era as a *pink boy* in the Lavender Conspiracy. Her father's brilliant, gentile, liberal, lawyerly professorial voice is the fault-line of democracy. One who is physically reserved but also one who nicknames his children and wife. One who is filled with affection but does not extend it through the physical.

Her father tells her, "Liberty and equality. are incompatible. This is the first contradiction you need to know. It describes the fault line in America and in its Constitution." His belief that "the preservation of a way of life that had its roots in the traditions of scholarship rather than the accidents of power" remains a central force in this collection.

Contradiction, fluidity and plurality of narrative, always present in her work, prove her agile and curious mind always on the take.

"Liberty is for the owners. Equality, the masses, or slaves. The troubling underbelly of these concepts is that most labor is equally and inherently unjust. A version of the plantation and prison. And I am not just talking about women, prostitution, cleaning services."

What is stunning about Fanny Howe's commentary on the 20th century is how we got where we are today. We see the clear headed and concise outlining of historical and institutionalized, systematized racism of our founding fathers by aligning it with a scientific method of oppression. Ultimately, how can this not be tied to the dismissal of the poor and the disregard for our planet? Her prediction is typically unpopular and weirdly accurate: "There will come a day when the poor and the old will be the only animals who know how to live on the earth."

Later she asks, who will care? What is the answer, "every rock and tree." There is in the world, the world of the unseen- the witness- which is the poet, but it is also eternal. The entire book is a recapitulation – to use her word- 'backward thinking' going over the finished thing again, but now including the self and the present moment in it. She calls it a 'negative presence' I call it a kind of holy calling to reimagine the past in the present. An example of the recapitulation is an entire page devoted to stamps from the 19th and 20th century with hand writing written slantwise over the page, an intimacy over history, masculinity, territory and most of all Victorian patriarchy.

Some of her father's letters are written in French peppered with Cambridge, American and teenage slang. Her father's awareness of how various people speak, their nuances, their codes reveal economic and cultural bias and position him to inform her poetic voice.

From a letter written on the 4th of July in 1957- "So if you feel dreary - as perhaps you do - remember that all would not have been cheer and rosiness at 58. I'm afraid it's the old story - life and affection are demanding and often frustrating." As I write this at his age now, I am feeling sympathetic to a man who has realized that 'life and affection are demanding and frustrating' and often one may feel defeated. What is striking about the father is that although he may have not been affectionate, he was devoted, writing to Howe every day at the summer camp where she was sent to learn French. It is a devotion that even now lives in her communion with him.

The book ends with a paper her father wrote outlining the legal and constitutional background of the Civil Rights Movement. In this particularly timely paper written in 1965, Mark DeWolfe Howe, a professor of law at Harvard, points out that federalism creates problems for the law. This book is a love story and a homage to this brilliant, kind man, and the conflicted city of Boston in which he lived in the 20th century.

Howe writes of her own frustration in putting the book together: "It was like trying to do an autopsy on the unconscious, the evidence being what was not revealed." How lucky we are that this self-examination took place. Toward the end of the book, Fanny Howe re-writes her father's obituary. The images of the snow he shoveled, and a thought of a sparrow underscore humility and beauty so persistent in her work. "The snow he had shoveled lay piled on the lawn. It blew here and there into colorful dust and gems. How cold it must be in the sky, thought a little sparrow."

EILEEN CLEARY

Review: *The Land of Mild Light* by Rafael Cadenas
Arrowsmith Books, 2021

Arrowsmith press, and editor Nidia Hernández have gathered selected poems from Rafael Cadenas, one of Venezuela's most eminent and lionized living poets, into the collection *The Land of Mild Light*. This volume represents Cardenas' work over the past six decades. The works are translated by seventeen poets originally from Jamaica, Scotland, England, Venezuela, Aruba and the United States of America, signaling the wide reach and appeal of this verse.

Throughout his writing career, Cadenas has been concerned with providing solace, encouragement, realistic reflection, humanism, and in the backdrop of political exile. (He was exiled to Trinidad for being a Communist.) His devout love of language illuminates truth, stripped bare and unpretentious.

Hyperbole and a pervading sense of inadequacy penetrate much of this work as demonstrated by these lines from "Defeat":

> I who have never had a trade
> who before any competitor have felt weak
> who have lost the best qualifcations for life
> who as soon as I arrive at a place already want to leave

Poets are perhaps especially susceptible to experiencing the sense of defeat, or failure, and to finding eventual accord with them. So it is not surprising, though it is refreshing to read Cadenas' epistolary to "Failure:"

> What I took for victory is only smoke.
> Failure, rock bottom language, trail from a different more demanding
>   place, your handwriting is diffcult to make out.
> When you put your mark on my forehead, I never thought about
>   the message you were bringing...

French-born American literary critic George Steiner said, "Without translation we would be living in provinces bordering on silence." We are fortunate that some of this silence has been breached in this collection, so clearly smitten with language. In these selected poems, Cardenas demands of his words, "terrifying exactitude. " He creates a spell which becomes an incantation to words in his poem, "Ars Poetica:"

Let each word carry what it says.
Let it be the tremor holding.
Let it keep like a heartbeat.

I encourage you to enter into *The Land of Mild Light,* which in its openess and intimacy, is as close as most of us can come to sitting across from this poet in a neighborhood café, conversing about poetry itself. Perhaps conversing about what remains after the facade is removed from verse, about "Just the clean work./Only the hidden splendor."

CONTRIBUTORS' NOTES

JONATHAN B. AIBEL is a poet who spends his days wrestling software to the ground as an engineer specializing in quality and testing. His poems have been published, or will soon appear, in *Ocean State Review, Soundings East, Pangyrus, Sweet Tree Review, Rogue Agent, Main Street Rag,* and elsewhere. He has studied with Lucie Brock-Broido, David Ferry and Barbara Helfgott Hyett. Jonathan lives in Concord, MA with his family.

LISA ALLEN's work has appeared in *Bacopa Literary Review* (2018, 2019), *Midway Journal* (2019), *Lily Poetry Review* (2019), *3Elements Review* (2019), and *December Magazine* (2020), and the anthologies *Listen to Your Mother: What She Said Then, What We're Saying Now* (2015), *Feckless Cunt* (2018), and *Dine* (2020). She holds MFAs in Creative Nonfiction and Poetry, both from The Solstice Low-Residency MFA in Creative Writing Program, where she was a Michael Steinberg Fellow. She has been nominated for a Pushcart Prize (2019, 2020) and is a co-founder of the virtual creative space The Notebooks Collective, as well as a founding co-editor of the anthology series Maximum Tilt.

JENNIFER BARBER's new collection, *The Sliding Boat Our Bodies Made*, is forthcoming from The Word Works in 2022. Her poems have recently appeared or are forthcoming in the *Paris Review, Ruminate,* and *Broadsided*, and her previous books are *Works on Paper* (2016), *Given Away* (2012), and *Rigging the Wind* (2003). She will serve as poet laureate of Brookline, Mass, from 2021 to 2024.

NATALKA BILOTSERKIVETS's work, known for lyricism and the quiet power of despair, became hallmarks of Ukraine's literary life of the 1980s. The collections *Allergy* (1999) and *Central Hotel* (2004) were the winners of Book of the Year contests in 2000 and 2004 respectively. In the West, she's mostly known on the strength of a handful of widely translated poems, while the better part of her oeuvre remains unknown. She lives and works in Kyiv. Her poem, "We'll Not Die in Paris," became the hymn of the post-Chornobyl generation of young Ukrainians that helped topple the Soviet Union.

DANTE BISS-GRAYSON is a Native American artist who had to find himself again after many years overseas in the war zone. Upon return to the States, he started his studio with the hopes to express the trauma of war, and find a platform to continually express himself, externalize the trauma, and eventually, hopefully help others. He creates artwork that pushes the boundaries of varying mediums, such as painting, holographic sculpture, poetry, and Fashion Design. He paints, sculpts, writes, and designs, trying to find the best platform to express and convey thought and emotion.

JAY BRECKER works and writes in southern California. His poems are forthcoming or have appeared in *Rattle Poets Respond, Permafrost, Ocean State Review, The Inflectionist Review, South 85 Journal, I-70 Review, RHINO Poetry,* and elsewhere. His manuscript, *A Ceiling is a Wall Seeking*, was a semi-finalist for the 2020 Wheeler Prize for Poetry.

M.P. CARVER is a poet and visual artist from Salem, MA. She is an editor at Yes-No Press, miCrO-Founder of the journal *Molecule: a tiny lit mag*, former Poetry Editor of *Soundings East*, and Director of the 2021 Massachusetts Poetry Festival. Find out more at mpcarver.com.

SAM CHA is from Korea. He earned an MFA at UMass Boston. A 2017 recipient of the St. Boltoph's Club Emerging Artists Prize, his work has appeared in *apt, Assay, Best New Poets 2016, Boston Review, DIAGRAM, Memorious,* and Missouri Review. His chapbook, *American Carnage,* was published by Portable Press @ Yo-Yo Labs in 2018. His full-length collection of cross-genre work, *The Yellow Book,* was published by [PANK] Books in 2020. Sam lives and writes in Cambridge, MA.

WILLY CONLEY, a former biomedical photographer, has photos featured in the books *Listening Through the Bone, The Deaf Heart, No Walls of Stone,* and *Deaf World.* Other publications: *American Photographer, Arkansas Review, Baltimore Sun, Carolina Quarterly, Big Muddy, Folio,* and *34th Parallel.* Conley is a professor of Theatre Arts at Gallaudet University, the world's only liberal arts university for deaf and hard-of-hearing students.

MARGARITA CRUZ recently received her MFA in Creative Writing from Northern Arizona University. She is currently a columnist for Flagstaff Live! and an assistant editor for Tolsun Books. Her works have been featured in *[PANK] Magazine, Chapter House Journal,* and *Susquehanna Review.*

ADAM DAY is the author of *Left-Handed Wolf* (LSU Press, 2020), and of *Model of a City in Civil War* (Sarabande Books), and the recipient of a Poetry Society of America Chapbook Fellowship for *Badger, Apocrypha,* and of a PEN Award. His work has appeared in *APR, Boston Review, Fence, Bomb, Kenyon Review,* and elsewhere. He is the publisher of *Action, Spectacle.*

SARAH DECKRO's poetry has been published by *Persephone's Daughters, Francis House, Gordon Square Review, Kaaterskill Basin Literary Journal, Curating Alexandria, Red Earth Review* and in the anthologies *An Outbreak of Peace* and *Dreamers Anthology.* Her photography has appeared in *Pidgeonholes, The Esthetic Apostle, Camas Magazine, Waxwing, The Bookends Review, Arkana Magazine* and *A Room of Her Own Foundation.*

FRANCES DONOVAN's chapbook *Mad Quick Hand of the Seashore* was named a finalist in the 31st Lambda Literary Awards. Her poetry and interviews have appeared in *The Rumpus, Heavy Feather Review, SWWIM, Solstice, Borderlands: Texas Poetry Review,* and elsewhere. She holds an MFA in poetry from Lesley University. She once drove a bulldozer in an LGBTQ+ Pride parade while wearing a bustier. You can find her online at www.gardenofwords.com. Twitter: @okelle.

CARLA DRYSDALE's poetry books are *All Born Perfect* (Kelsay Books, 2019), *Inheritance* (Finishing Line Press, 2016) and *Little Venus* (Tightrope Books, 2009). Poems appear in *Cleaver, Literary Mama, Literary Review of Canada, The Fiddlehead, PRISM International* and many other journals. Nominated for a Pushcart Prize and Bettering American Poetry recognition, she received *PRISM's* 2014 Earle Birney poetry prize. She is currently working on another book of poems and a novel set in northern Wales. A Canadian, she lives in France and works at the United Nations in Geneva. More at www.carladrysdale.com

JENNIFER F. is a fiction writer and journalist born in New Jersey and based in California. She writes about food for publications around the world and has an MA in Creative Writing from the University of California, Davis.

JENNIFER FRANKLIN is the author of *No Small Gift* (Four Way Books, 2018) and *If Some God Shakes Your House* (Four Way Books, 2023). Her publications include *American Poetry Review*, *Boston Review*, *Gettysburg Review*, *JAMA*, *Love's Executive Order*, *The Nation*, *New England Review*, *Paris Review*, "poem-a-day" on poets.org, and *Prairie Schooner*. She teaches in Manhattanville's MFA program and the Hudson Valley Writers Center, where she serves as Program Director. She lives in New York City.

JENNIFER L. FREED's poems have appeared in various journals including *Atlanta Review*, *Atticus Review*, *Naugatuck River Review*, *Rust + Moth*, *The Worcester Review*, and *Zone 3*. Her chapbook *These Hands Still Holding* (Finishing Line), was a finalist in the 2013 New Women's Voices contest. She was awarded the 2020 Samuel Washington Allen Prize from the New England Poetry Club, and has recently completed a full-length manuscript based on the repercussions of her mother's cerebral hemorrhage. Please visit jfreed.weebly.com.

VIOLETA GARCIA-MENDOZA is a writer, photographer, and teacher in love with the natural world around her. She lives with her family in Western Pennsylvania.

JENNY GRASSL's poems have appeared in *The Boston Review*, *Tupelo Quarterly*, *Rhino Poetry*, *Phantom Drift*, *The Massachusetts Review*, *Ocean State Review*, *Lana Turner*, and other journals. Her work was published in a National Poetry Month feature of *Iowa Review*, and *Green Mountains Review* will publish her poem in an upcoming issue. She lives in Cambridge, Massachusetts.

JANE POIRIER HART, a finalist in the 2018 Elyse Wolf Prize, holds an MFA in Writing from Vermont College of Fine Arts and was named Poetry Fellow at the Writers' Room of Boston. Her work has appeared in print and online journals, including *The Southern Poetry Review*, *The Worcester Review*, *The Ocean State Review*, *The Plath Poetry Project*, *MER Vox Folio* and *Autumn Sky Daily Poetry*. She makes her home in the suburbs of Boston.

CAROL HOBBS is a poet and educator with Massachusetts Public Schools. Her work has appeared in journals and anthologies throughout the United States and Canada. Her recent book, *New-found-land*, available through Main Street Rag in North Carolina, received honorable mention for the Sheila Margaret Motton Book Prize with the NEPC, and a New England PEN Discovery Prize.

RICHARD HOFFMAN has published four volumes of poetry, *Without Paradise; Gold Star Road*, winner of the Barrow Street Press Poetry Prize and the Sheila Margaret Motton Award from The New England Poetry Club; *Emblem*; and *Noon until Night*, winner of the 2018 Massachusetts Book Award for Poetry. His other books include the memoirs *Half the House* and *Love & Fury*, and the story collection *Interference and Other Stories*.

LAURA REECE HOGAN is the author of *Litany of Flights* (Paraclete Press, 2020), winner of the Paraclete Poetry Prize, the chapbook *O Garden-Dweller* (Finishing Line Press), and the nonfiction book *I Live, No Longer I* (Wipf & Stock). A Pushcart Prize and Best of the Net nominee, she has contributed to *Whale Road Review*, *Santa Fe Literary Review*, *Dappled Things*, *Cumberland River Review*, *The Cresset*, *EcoTheo Review*, *Poets Reading the News*, and other publications.

AMANDA HOPE lives in eastern Massachusetts with her partner and cats. A graduate of Colgate University and Simmons College, she works as a librarian. Her poems have recently appeared in publications including *The Shallow Ends*, *Impossible Archetype*, *TIMBER*, *honey & lime*, and *Barrow Street*. Her chapbook, *The Museum of Resentments*, was published by Paper Nautilus in 2020.

ERIC E. HYETT is a poet and Japanese translator from Brookline, MA. His poems, essays, and translations have most recently appeared in *The Georgia Review*, *Granta*, *Modern Poetry in Translation*, *Pendemics*, *Tokyo Poetry Journal*, and *World Literature Today*. His translation (with Spencer Thurlow) of "Sonic Peace " by Kiriu Minashita made the shortlists for the 2018 National Translation Award and the 2018 Lucien Stryk Asian Translation Prize. Eric's first collection of poetry, "Aporia" will be published in September 2021 by Lily Poetry Review Books.

SHELAGH POWERS JOHNSON graduated with an MFA from American University's Creative Writing program and is an English professor at Bowie State University. Her work has previously appeared in *Portland Review*, *apt*, *Typishly*, *Luna Luna Magazine*, *Ravishly*, the *Grace and Gravity* anthologies, *Night Train*, *Avatar Literary Review*, and *Clackamas Literary Review*, among others. She lives outside Baltimore with her husband and daughter.

EDWARD JOSEPH KAITZ started producing art when he was bedridden for three months with rheumatic fever as a middle schooler. His inspiration is drawn from internal suffering, feelings, and obscurity. He found this inspiration referenced well in the works of Leonard Baskin, Jose Luis Cuervas, and Francis Bacon. His illness led him on an existential journey to find out why we are here. His art is a process of understanding how he came to be here, and where he is going. While not a treatise, it is a dharma for living, imperfect and humble.

ALI KINSELLA has been translating from Ukrainian for eight years. Her published works include essays, poetry, monographs, and subtitles to various films. She holds an MA from Columbia University, where she wrote a thesis on the intersection of feminism and nationalism in small states. A former Peace Corps volunteer, Ali lived in Ukraine for nearly five years. She is currently in Chicago, where she also sometimes works as a baker.

K. T. LANDON is the author of *Orange, Dreaming* (Five Oaks Press, 2017). Her poetry has appeared in *North American Review*, *Narrative*, and *Best New Poets 2017*, and her work has been nominated for the Pushcart Prize and Best of the Net anthology.

WALTER LAWN writes poetry and short fiction. His work has been published in *Every Day Fiction*, *River Poets Journal*, and the anthology *Unclaimed Baggage*. Walter is a disaster recovery planner and lives outside of Philadelphia.

JENNA LE (jennalewriting.com) is a daughter of Vietnamese refugees who was born and raised in Minnesota. She is a New York City-based physician and educator and the author of two poetry collections, *Six Rivers* (NYQ Books, 2011) and *A History of the Cetacean American Diaspora* (Indolent Books, 2018), the latter of which was an Elgin Awards Second Place winner. Her poems have appeared in *AGNI*, *Denver Quarterly*, *Los Angeles*

Review, Massachusetts Review, Michigan Quarterly Review, Pleiades, Poet Lore, Verse Daily, and *West Branch.* Her visual art has appeared in *Jubilat, Lantern Review, Mom Egg Review, Pulse,* and *West Trestle Review.*

DAVID DODD LEE is the author of ten books of poetry, including *Animalities* (Four Way Books, 2014) and *Orphan, Indiana* (Akron, 2010), as well as a forthcoming book of collages, erasure poems, and new original poems (*Unlucky Animals*, Wolfson Press, 2022). Visual art has appeared recently at *Off the Coast, The Hunger, Tupelo Quarterly, Rougarou, The Indianapolis Review, Packingtown Review, House Mountain Review,* and *Watershed Review.* An essay, with artwork, is forthcoming in Rose Metal Press's *A Field Guide to Graphic Literature* (2022). He is Associate Professor of English at Indiana University South Bend.

KALI LIGHTFOOT lives in Salem, MA. Her poems and reviews of poetry books have appeared in journals and anthologies, including *Feminine Rising, Lavender Review, Broadsides to Books, Star 82 Review,* and *Gyroscope.* Kali's work has been nominated twice for Pushcart Prize, and once for Best of the Net. She earned an MFA at Vermont College of Fine Arts, and her debut collection of poems was published by CavanKerry Press in April, 2021. Find Kali at www.kali-lightfoot.com

JULIA LISELLA's books include *Always* (WordTech Editions, 2014), *Terrain* (WordTech Editions, 2007), and a chapbook, *Love Song Hiroshima* (Finishing Line Press, 2004). Her poems are widely anthologized, and appear in *Ploughshares, Paterson Literary Review, Mom Egg Review, Nimrod, Exit 7, Ocean State Review* and others. She writes on modernist women writers, teaches American literature at Regis College, and co-curates the Italian American Writers Association (IAWA) Reading Series in Boston.

JENNIFER MARTELLI is the author of *My Tarantella* (Bordighera Press), awarded an Honorable Mention from the Italian American Studies Association, selected as a 2019 "Must Read" by the Massachusetts Center for the Book, and named a finalist for the Housatonic Book Award. Her chapbook, *After Bird*, was the winner of the Grey Book Press open reading, 2016. Her work has appeared in *Poetry, Thrush, West Trestle Review, Verse Daily, Iron Horse* Review (winner, Photo Finish contest), *The Sycamore Review,* and *Cream City Review.* Jennifer Martelli has twice received grants from the Massachusetts Cultural Council for her poetry. She is co-poetry editor for *Mom Egg Review* and co-curates the Italian-American Writers Series.

LIBBY MAXEY is a senior editor at *Literary Mama,* where she has been on staff since 2012. Her poems have appeared in *Emrys, THINK, Pirene's Fountain, Pinyon, Stoneboat, Crannóg* and elsewhere, and her first poetry collection, *Kairos,* won Finishing Line Press's 2018 New Women's Voices Chapbook Competition. Her nonliterary activities include singing classical repertoire, mothering two sons, enjoying the woods of Western Massachusetts, and administering the Department of Classics at Amherst College.

KIRSTEN MILES s is the National Director of the 30/30 Project at Tupelo Press and Regional Director of Tupelo Press Conferences. She founded the Tupelo Press Teen Writing Center in Charlottesville, Virginia, supporting teen writers and developing programming for scalable community support for writing as an art for teens. A bookmaker and member of a local letterpress non-profit with the Virginia Foundation for the Humanities, she enjoys exploring the very slow process of making books by hand, and the relationship of the book to its content. She is working on her first novel.

GLORIA MONAGHAN is a Professor of Humanities at Wentworth University. She has published five books of poetry: *Flawed* (Finishing Line Press), *Torero* (Nixes Mate), *The Garden* (Flutter Press), *False Spring* (Adelaide), and *Hydrangea* (Kelsay Books). Her poems have appeared in *Alexandria Quarterly, 2River, Adelaide, Aurorean, Chiron, Nixes-Mate, First Literary Review East*, among others. In 2018 her poem, "Into Grace" was nominated for the Pushcart Prize. Her book *False Spring* was nominated for the Griffin Prize.

JASON R. MONTGOMERY, or JRM, is a Chicano/Indigenous Californian writer, painter, and playwright from El Centro, California. He merges Indigenous Californian and Chicano designs and aesthetics to explore the history of US colonization while synthesizing a decolonized motif that honors the complicated heritage of the postcolonial subject. JRM's work has appeared in Split Lip Magazine, Storm Cellar, Ilanot Review, and other publications. He is also a 2021-23 Poets Laureate for East Hampton, Mass.

HEATHER NELSON is a poet, teacher, mother, and recovering attorney who has lived in Cambridge since 1995. She is the Writers' Room Coordinator for 826 Boston at the John D. O'Bryant School of Mathematics and Science, where she helps many students find their writing voices and create great work. Her own work has been published in *Main Street Rag, Lily Poetry Review, Spoon River Poetry Review, The Somerville Times, Constellations, The Ekphrastic Review,* and *The Compassion Anthology*.

STEPHEN NELSON's last book was a Xerolage of visual poetry called *Arcturian Punctuation* (Xexoxial Editions). He has exhibited visual poetry and published prose and poetry internationally for a number of years. He lives by a burn in Central Scotland with a cat called Amma and is currently writing a YA sci-fi fantasy novel while drinking lots of Brazilian coffee.

BARBARA O'BYRNE is a Literacy Education professor living in Charleston, WV where she directs a site of the National Writing Project. Her fiction has appeared in *Perigee Publication for the Art, Flash Fiction,* and *The Citron Review*. When not writing, she can be found on a bicycle, exploring the forests of West Virginia.

MIRIAM O'NEAL's, *The Body Dialogues* was published by Lily Poetry Review Books in January, 2020. *We Start with What We're Given* (Kelsay Books) came out in 2018. Runner-up for the 2020 Princemere Prize, O'Neal is a 2019 Pushcart nominee and a Poet of Note in the Disquiet International Poetry competition. Recent work has appeared in *Nixes Mate Review, North Dakota Quarterly*. Translations of Italian poet, Alda Merini, appeared in *On the Seawall* in Fall 2019.

DZVINIA ORLOWSKY, Pushcart Prize poet, translator, and a founding editor of Four Way Books, is author of six poetry collections published by Carnegie Mellon University Press including *Bad Harvest*, a 2019 Massachusetts Book Awards "Must Read" in Poetry. Her translation from the Ukrainian of Alexander Dovzhenko's novella, *The*

Enchanted Desna, was published by House Between Water Press in 2006, and in 2014, Dialogos published Jeff Friedman's and her co-translation of *Memorials: A Selection* by Polish poet Mieczslaw Jastrun for which she and Friedman were awarded a 2016 National Endowment for the Arts Literature Translation Fellowship. Ali Kinsella and Dzvinia's book of co-translations from the Ukrainian titled *Eccentric Days of Hope and Sorrow: Selected Poems by Natalka Bilotserkivets* is forthcoming from Lost Horse Press in fall 2021.

CHRISTIE PAGE is a resilient warrior. Art was first a distraction, a way to escape from the torment of her mind and pour thoughts onto paper, whether through poetry or painting. Soon she realized she could process her pain, one memory at a time and leave those memories trapped on the pages she painted on. She began to feel lighter. She started to shed. She started to grow. Anger gave way to empathy and empathy gave way to forgiveness. Forgiveness of self. And that gave way to grace and allowing herself grace.

ASHLEY PARKER OWENS is an Appalachian writer, poet, and artist living in Richmond, Kentucky. She has an MFA in Creative Writing from Eastern Kentucky University and an MFA in Visual Arts from Rutgers University.

NATASHA PEPPERL's work has appeared or is forthcoming in *Appalachian Review, The Meadow, The Maynard, The Anti-Languorous Project,* and elsewhere. She hosts *Just As Special,* a foster care podcast focused on diversity, and is the daughter of an Iranian refugee. Read more of Natasha's poetry at CeremoniesOfFamily.com.

ANNE ELEZABETH PLUTO   Professor of Literature and Theatre at Lesley University in Cambridge, MA where she is the artistic director and one of the founders of the Oxford Street Players, the university's Shakespeare troupe.. She was a member of the Boston small press scene in the late 1980s and is one of the founders and editors at *Nixes Mate Review*. Recent publications include *The Buffalo Evening News, Unlikely Stories: Episode IV, Mat Hat Lit, Pirene's Fountain, The Enchanting Verses Literary Review, Mockingheart Review, Yellow Chair Review, Levure Litteraire – numero 12, The Naugatuck River Review, Tuesday: An Art Project, Muddy River Review,* and *Mom Egg Review,* with forthcoming work in *Fulcrum.* Her most recent poetry collection, *The Deepest Part of Dark,* was published by Unlikely Books in 2020.

ERWIN PONCE is at work on a poetry manuscript called *Pilipinas, or; Ending up in Modern Day Metro Manila.* His poems appear in *Eastlit, Asian American Literary Review, TAYO Literary Magazine,* and *Cha: An Asian Literary Journal.* He holds an MFA from Emerson College and works at a public library.

ERIC ROY's poems have appeared or are forthcoming from *Bennington Review, Green Mountains Review, Salamander, Salt Hill, Sugar House Review, Third Coast* and elsewhere. His debut chapbook, *All Small Planes,* is available from Lily Poetry. His hybrid piece, "Origin Story," has been nominated for inclusion in Best Small Fictions 2021 and can be read here https://www.ruminatemagazine.com/blogs/ruminate-blog/origin-story

MEGGIE ROYER is a Midwestern writer, domestic violence advocate, and the Founder and Editor-in-Chief of *Persephone's Daughters,* a literary and arts journal for abuse survivors. She has won numerous awards for her work and has been nominated several times for the Pushcart Prize. She thinks there is nothing better in this world than a finished poem.

ZEDEKIAH SCHILD is a painter and sculptor living and working in San Francisco, California.

J.D.SCRIMGEOUR is the author of four poetry collections, including *Lifting the Turtle* and *Festival*. His collection of bilingual poetry, 香蕉面包/*Banana Bread*, will be published by Nixes Mate Press in Fall 2021. He won the AWP Award for Nonfiction for his second book of nonfiction, *Themes for English B: A Professor's Education In & Out of Class*.

NEIL SILBERBLATT is the founder / director of Voices of Poetry. He has curated and presented more than 400 poetry events at various venues in MA, CT, NY & NJ. Neil's poems have appeared in numerous literary journals including *Plume Poetry Journal*, *Mom Egg Review*, *Tiferet Journal*, *American Journal of Poetry*, and *Tikkun Daily*, also the anthologies, *Collateral Damage* (Pirene's Fountain) and *Culinary Poems* (Glass Lyre Press). His most recent poetry collection, *Past Imperfect* (Nixes Mate Books, 2018), was nominated for the Mass. Book Award in Poetry, and he has been nominated several times for a Pushcart Prize.

ANDY SMART earned his MFA from the Solstice Low-Residency Program at Pine Manor College, where he was the 2018 Michael Steinberg Creative Nonfiction Fellow. His work has appeared in the *American Journal of Poetry*, *Salamander*, *Glassworks*, and elsewhere. Andy was a 2019 Pushcart Prize nominee. His chapbook *Blue Horse Suite* is available from Kattywompus Press, and his first book, *The More You Hate Me*, a memoir in essays, is due out in 2022 from Unsolicited Press.

LISA J. SULLIVAN is a Massachusetts native who holds an MFA in Poetry from the Solstice Low-Residency MFA Program, where she was a Kurt Brown Memorial Fellow. Her work has appeared in *The American Journal of Poetry*, *The Comstock Review*, *The Chaffin Journal*, and elsewhere. She is an associate poetry editor for Lily Poetry Review Books and a poetry editor for *Pink Panther Magazine*. Lisa is also a visual artist and teaches poetry workshops at the Plymouth Center for the Arts.

JW SUMMERISLE lives in the English East Midlands and once appeared in *Memoir Mixtapes* with a poem about Courtney Love's 'Doll Parts'.

SHARON TRACEY is a poet and editor, and author of two full-length poetry collections: *Chroma: Five Centuries of Women Artists* (Shanti Arts Publishing, 2020) and *What I Remember Most is Everything* (All Caps Publishing, 2017). Her poems have appeared in *Terrain.org*, *The Worcester Review*, *Mom Egg Review*, *SWWIM*, *The Ekphrastic Review*, and elsewhere. She lives and writes in western Massachusetts.

M. J. TURNER's poems have appeared in *Nixes Mate*, *Spillway*, *concīs*, and the *I-70 Review*. She lives in Massachusetts.

PETER URKOWITZ lives in Salem, Massachusetts where he works at the college library. He's published poems and art in *Meat for Tea*, *The Valley Review*, *Oddball Magazine*, *Sextant*, and *Lily Poetry Review*. His *Fake Zodiac Signs* are published in a chapbook from Meat for Tea Press.

LOU VARGO was born and raised in Detroit. He and his family live in Nashville, Tennessee. He is a certified sommelier and makes his living in the wine business.

MID WALSH is a poet, singer, athlete, husband, and grandfather living near the ocean. With an English BA from Yale University and an MBA, he has conducted careers as a carpenter, a hi-tech executive, and a yoga studio owner. His poetry renders his life experiences into the music of language. He lives with his wife and two wise cats near the seashore just south of Boston.

JIM WILLIS grew up in Shreveport, Louisiana and graduated from Northwestern State College in Natchitoches. He has a Masters in English from Tulane University. He has published poems in *The Tulane Review, DMQ Review, Ekphrasis, Melic Review, Snowy Egret, Terrain.org*, and *Hawai'i Pacific Review*. He won the 2003 Frith Press Open Chapbook Competition with a collection called *The Darwin Point*. He recently moved to Apalachicola, Florida to be near his daughter, Ashley.

ROBERT WILSON is an artist, tutor, and writer living in Cape Haze, Florida, and Fort Wayne, Indiana. His poems have appeared in journals including the *Pinyon Review* and the *Poetica Review*, and his chapbook *A Charity of Blue* was published by Yavanika Press. After three surgeries his vision has mercifully been restored.

www.ingramcontent.com/pod-product-compliance
Lightning Source LLC
Chambersburg PA
CBHW072156100526
44589CB00015B/2250